EYEWITNESS TRAVEL TOP 10

VENICE

GILLIAN PRICE

Left **Piazza San Marco** Right **Façade, Doge's Palace**

LONDON, NEW YORK,
MELBOURNE, MUNICH AND DELHI
www.dk.com

Produced by
Book Creation Services Ltd, London

Reproduced by Colourscan, Singapore
Printed and bound in China by Leo
Paper Products Ltd

First published in Great Britain in
2002
by Dorling Kindersley Limited
80 Strand, London WC2R 0RL
A Penguin Company

**Copyright 2002, 2007 © Dorling
Kindersley Limited, London**

**Reprinted with revisions 2003, 2005,
2007**

A CIP catalogue record is available from
the British Library.

ISBN: 978 1 40531 697 2

Within each Top 10 list in this book, no
hierarchy of quality or popularity is
implied. All 10 are, in the editor's
opinion, of roughly equal merit.

Contents

Venice's Top 10

Cover: Front – **Corbis:** Mark L Stephenson main; **DK Images:** John Heseltine cl; Demetrio Carrasco bl.
Back – **DK Images:** Demetrio Carrasco tc; John Heseltine tl, tr. Spine – **DK Images:** Demetrio Carrasco.

Left **Ballroom, Museo Correr** Right **Gondola traghetto ride**

Left **Mercerie shops** Right **Venice Carnival**

VENICE'S TOP 10

🔟 Venice Highlights

The uniquely romantic city of Venice was built entirely on water and has managed to survive into the 21st century without cars. Narrow alleyways and canals pass between sumptuous palaces and magnificent churches, colourful neighbourhood markets and quiet backwaters, unchanged for centuries. Few cities possess such an awesome line-up of sights for visitors.

Basilica San Marco

Venice's fairytale cathedral is pure Byzantine in essence, while its façade and interior have been embellished with resplendent mosaics and exquisite works of art through the ages *(see pp8–11)*.

Doge's Palace

This was the powerhouse of the city's rulers for nearly 900 years. Passing through a maze of rooms gives visitors an insight into the sumptuous lifestyle that so often accompanied state affairs *(see pp12–15)*.

Piazza San Marco

Elegance and opulence sit side by side in what Napoleon named "the most elegant drawing room in Europe". This magnificent square is adorned with monuments that give testimony to Venice's glorious past *(see pp16–19)*.

Grand Canal

The city's majestic watercourse swarms with all manner of boats, while its embankments boast a dazzling succession of palaces dating back as early as the 13th century *(see pp20–23)*.

Map labels: Cannaregio, Canal Grande, Santa Croce, Dorsoduro, CMPO S. SIMEON PROFETA, LISTA DEI BARI, CAMPO NAZARIO SAURO, CAMPO SAN GIACOMO DELL'ORIO, CAMPO DEI TOLENTINI, FMTA MINOTTO, CAMPO SAN STIN, CAMPO D. FRARI, CAMPO SAN ROCCO, CAMPO SAN TOMA, CAMPO SAN PANTALON, CAMPO SANTA MARGHERITA, CAMPO DEI CARMINI, R. T. SANT'APONAL, CAMPO SAN BARNABA, CPO SAN SAMUELE, CAMPO SAN VIDAL, CAMPO D. CARITA, R. T. A. FOSCARINI, Ponte dell'Accademia

10 Peggy Guggenheim Collection
Italy's leading museum for 20th-century European and American art, the collection is housed in a one-floor palace on the Grand Canal (see pp34–5).

9 Campo Santa Margherita
A wonderful square, bustling with life day and night thanks to its market stalls and outdoor cafés. An added bonus is its many architectural styles (see pp32–3).

8 Island of Torcello
Escape the crowds in the city with a ferry ride over the vast expanse of the lagoon to this peaceful, lush island, the site of Venice's original settlement (see pp30–31).

7 Rialto Market
This Mediterranean fresh produce market has enlivened this quayside since medieval times and is arguably still the best market in the world (see pp28–9).

250 ⌐————— yards ¬ 0 ⌐ metres ————— ¬ 250

5 Accademia Galleries
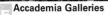
An unsurpassed collection of Venetian paintings, with masterpieces by Titian, Bellini and Giorgione. A must, not only for art lovers (see pp24–5).

6 Santa Maria Gloriosa dei Frari
A Gothic interior with grandiose works of art lies in store behind this church's brick façade (see pp26–7).

For guided tours around Venice See p136

7

Basilica San Marco

This breathtaking Byzantine basilica, dominating Piazza San Marco (see pp16–19), was constructed in such ornate fashion for two reasons: as an embodiment of the Venetian Republic's power and as a fitting resting place for St Mark. Serving as the Doges' chapel, coronations, funerals and processions were held here, gloriously framed by more than 4,000 sq m (43,000 sq ft) of mosaics, eastern treasures and 500 columns dating from the 3rd century.

Basilica San Marco façade

⊙ Visit the basilica at dusk, when the rays of the setting sun beautifully light up the façade.

Binoculars are a great help for examining mosaics high up on the walls.

- Piazza San Marco
- Map Q5
- 041 522 52 05
- Open: Basilica May–Sep: 9:45am–5:30pm Mon–Sat; Oct–Apr: 9:45am–4:30pm Mon–Sat; 2–4om Sun & hols; Museum and Loggia Cavalli Apr–Oct: 9:45am–5pm, Nov–Mar: 9:45am–4pm Mon–Sun; Pala d'Oro and Treasury; May–Sep: 9:45am–5:30pm Mon–Sat; Oct–Apr: 9:45am–4:30pm Mon–Sat, 2–5pm Sun & public hols; Oct–Mar: 9:45am– 4pm Mon–Sat, 2–4pm Sun & public hols
- Admission: Basilica free; Museum €3; Pala d'Oro €1.50; Treasury €2
- No disabled access beyond ground floor
- Free guided visits – book two days ahead on www.alata.it
- Bookshop

Top 10 Features

1. Western Façade
2. Atrium Mosaics
3. Flooring
4. Pala d'Oro
5. Ascension Dome
6. Pentecost Dome
7. Basilica Museum
8. Loggia dei Cavalli
9. The Tetrarchs
10. Treasury

Western Façade

A marvellous succession of domes, columns, arches and spires, interspersed with marble statues, screens and glittering mosaics, greets tourists in Piazza San Marco. The northernmost arch houses mosaics dating from the 13th century, which depict the basilica itself. Other mosaics are 17th- and 18th-century copies.

Atrium Mosaics

These glorious mosaics *(above)* of precious gold-leaf over glass tiles were created in the Byzantine tradition by expert craftsmen, and give detailed accounts of the Old Testament. The 13th-century cupola's concentric circles recount 24 episodes from *Genesis*, including the Creation and Adam and Eve.

Flooring

The paving is a mosaic masterpiece of multicoloured stones on uneven levels, evocative of the sea. Geometrical designs sit alongside animal shapes.

For more Venice churches See pp38–9

Pala d'Oro

The dazzling jewel-encrusted gold screen was commissioned in Constantinople in 976 but frequently added to at later dates. It boasts 250 panels bearing 1,927 authentic gems and *cloisonné* plaques.

Pentecost Dome

Probably the first dome of the basilica to be adorned with mosaics, it is illustrated with the descent of the Holy Ghost *(above)*, seen as a flame over the heads of the 12 Apostles.

Basilica Museum

Inside the fascinating museum are the famed quartet of horses crafted from bronze and covered in gold. Booty from the Fourth Crusade, these triumphal Graeco-Roman equine figures originally graced the Hippodrome in Constantinople. They have been restored to their former glory.

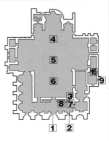

Basilica Floorplan

The Tetrarchs

The inspiration for these red porphyry rock figures from 4th-century Egypt is unknown. They may represent Saracens who, scheming to make off with treasure, poisoned each other and ended up as stone.

Treasury

The basilica's glittering riches include precious chalices of rock crystal enamelled by medieval silver- and goldsmiths and reliquaries from Venice's eastern conquests, including parts of the True Cross.

Loggia dei Cavalli

Replicas of the proud horses now in the museum stand on this wonderful balcony overlooking Piazza San Marco. Visitors can see the ancient lead gutter spouts, as well as clutches of columns, whose varied dimensions and decorative styles indicate their diverse origins.

Ascension Dome

The central dome has a spectacular array of early 13th-century mosaics, depicting the New Testament. *Christ in Glory* is shown above depictions of the Virtues.

Building the Basilica

Construction began on the first building in 829. However, during a revolt in 976, it was burned down and dismantled. The building we see today, a Greek cross layout surmounted by five domes, possibly modelled on the Church of the Holy Apostles in Constantinople, dates from 1071. The main architect is depicted over the central portal, biting his fingers in frustration over a building defect. The basilica became the city cathedral in 1807.

For more on Venice's San Marco district **See pp72–9**

Left **Museum horses** Centre left **Wall-slabs** Centre right **Altar columns** Right **Byzantine screens**

Basilica Architectural Features

1 Galleries
The airy catwalks over the body of the basilica reflect the eastern tradition of segregation in worship as they were exclusively for women. They are closed to visitors.

2 Stone Wall-slabs
Brick-faced until the 1100s, the walls were then covered with stone slabs from the East, sliced lengthways to produce a kaleidoscopic effect.

3 Romanesque Stone Carvings
The exquisite semi-circular stone carvings over the central doorway were executed between 1235–65 and still bear traces of their original colour.

4 The "Victory Bringer"
This revered Byzantine icon is given pride of place in the Madonna Nicopeia Chapel. Rumoured to have been executed by St Luke, it was carried into battle for its miraculous powers.

5 Baptistry
Aglow with 14th-century mosaic scenes of the life of St John, this is also home to the tomb of architect Sansovino (see p45). Closed to visitors.

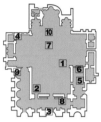

Basilica Floorplan

6 Zen Chapel
The sumptuous decoration in this small chapel was executed for the funeral of its namesake, Cardinal Zen, in 1521, in recognition of his gifts to the state. Closed to visitors.

7 Iconostasis
This elaborate screen separates the worship area of the chancel from the nave. Its eight columns are topped with Gothic-style statues of the Virgin and the Apostles, sculpted by the Delle Masegne brothers in 1394.

8 Byzantine Pierced Screens
Influenced by eastern architecture, delicate geometrical designs and lattice-work stone screens are featured on all three façades, in the atrium and loggia.

9 Porta dei Fiori
This doorway on the northern façade bears a 13th-century nativity scene surrounded by vines and Moorish arches.

10 Altar Columns
Four finely carved alabaster and marble columns support a canopy at the altar, beneath which lies the body of St Mark.

Porta dei Fiori

For more on Venice architects **See p45**

Venice's Top 10 Relics

1. Milk of the Virgin Mary, Basilica Treasury *(see p9)*
2. Blood of Christ, Basilica Treasury
3. Nail from the True Cross, Chiesa di San Pantalon *(see p39)*
4. Thorn from Christ's crown, Basilica Treasury
5. Body of St Mark, Basilica San Marco *(see pp8–9)*
6. Body of St Lucy, Chiesa di San Geremia
7. Three rocks used to stone St Stephen to death, Basilica Treasury
8. Skull of St John the Baptist, Basilica Treasury
9. Leg of St George, Basilica Treasury
10. Foot of St Catherine of Siena, Santi Giovanni e Paolo *(see p102)*

St Mark, Patron Saint of Venice

Although the well-loved saint of Byzantium, St Theodore, had been appointed protector of Venice by the Byzantine emperor, the fledgling republic felt in need of a saint of its own. In AD 828, two adroit Venetian merchants filched the body of St Mark from a monastery in Alexandria, ostensibly transporting it under layers of pork fat to conceal it from Muslim guards. The welcome in Venice was triumphant, and the story was recounted in countless paintings and mosaics. The remains, however, were mislaid for years, until an arm

Stealing St Mark's body

miraculously broke through a column in 1094 (marked by a small cross, left of the Altar of the Sacrament) in answer to a prayer. St Mark now rests in peace beneath the basilica's main altar. The ubiquitous winged lion representing St Mark could be found throughout the republic as the trademark of Venetian dominion: it is often shown with two paws in the sea and two on land, to symbolize the geography of Venice.

Medieval Venice, centred around Basilica San Marco

For more Venice churches **See pp38–9**

11

Doge's Palace

A magnificent combination of Byzantine, Gothic and Renaissance architecture, the Palazzo Ducale (Doge's Palace) was the official residence of the 120 doges who ruled Venice from 697 to 1797. A fortress-like structure stood here in the 9th century, to be replaced by the elegant Gothic version seen today, despite a string of fires in the 1500s. Artists such as Titian, Tintoretto and Bellini vied with each other to embellish the palace with painting and sculpture, not to mention architects Antonio Rizzo and Pietro Lombardo, the latter responsible for the ornate inner western façade.

Doge's Palace façade

🍴 A quiet modern café in the former stables on the ground floor serves snacks and drinks on water level.

🔎 Don't miss the Museo dell'Opera near the ticket office as it houses many original 14th-century façade capitals – those outside are mostly 19th-century copies.

• Piazza San Marco
• Map R5
• Open 9am–7pm daily (Nov–Mar 9am–5pm) (last admission 60 min before closing time); closed 1 Jan, 25 Dec
• Admission: €11 (includes admission to Museo Correr Complex)
• Secret Itineraries Tour: 041 520 90 70 (advance booking essential at palace or by phone); 9:55am, 10:45am & 11:35am daily in English; Admission: €12.50 plus €2.50 booking fee (includes palace)

Top 10 Features

1. Façade
2. Sala del Maggior Consiglio
3. Sala del Senato
4. Prisons
5. Ponte dei Sospiri
6. Scala d'Oro
7. Sala dello Scudo
8. Armoury
9. Porta della Carta
10. Doge's Apartments

Façade
Elegant twin façades face the piazzetta and the quayside. Pink-and-cream stonework and a loggia stand above an arcade of columns with 36 sculpted Istrian stone capitals.

Sala del Maggior Consiglio
The majestic Great Council Chamber is lined with canvases depicting Venetian victories and a cornice frieze of 76 doges – a black curtain represents traitor Marin Falier *(see p15)*.

Sala del Senato
The Senate members who met in this lavish hall *(above)* were nobles entrusted with debating war, foreign affairs and trade with the Doge. Time was measured by two clocks – one with a 24-hour face, the other with zodiac signs.

For more Venice palaces **See pp42–3**

Prisons

A fascinating maze of cells is linked by corridors and staircases on both sides of the canal. Famous inmate Casanova *(see p52)* made a dramatic escape across the roof in 1756. The "new prisons" were in use until the 1940s and feature poignant graffiti by internees.

Palace Guide

Rooms are labelled with explanatory panels in English and Italian and are spread over three floors and several wings. Follow the red arrows. Highly recommended is the Secret Itineraries Tour through chambers which were once used for administrative purposes and torture.

Sala dello Scudo

Enormous globes and painted wall maps showing the known world in 1762 make this room a must. The map of Eastern Asia traces Marco Polo's travels to China, complete with camels, rhinoceros and the mythical Uncharted Lands of the People Eaters.

Armoury

Fascinating, if spine-chilling, collection of beautifully crafted firearms, ceremonial weapons and suits of armour from East and West *(below)*. Among the war trophies is a Turkish standard brought back from the Battle of Lepanto (1571).

Ponte dei Sospiri

One of the world's most famous bridges, the "Bridge of Sighs" is an early 17th-century Baroque structure that crosses to the palace prisons. It would reputedly cause the condemned to "sigh" at their last glimpse of sky and sea.

Scala d'Oro

The sumptuous Golden Staircase, so-called for its Classical stucco decorations in 24-carat gold-leaf framing frescoes, led guests of honour to the second floor. Designed by Sansovino *(see p45)*, it was later completed by Scarpagnino in 1559.

Porta della Carta

The main entrance to the palace (now the visitors' exit) has a beautifully sculpted 1438 portal by the Bon family. It was named the "paper door" because edicts were posted here.

Doge's Apartments

The communicating rooms of the Doge's living quarters are furnished with rich brocades, impressive fireplaces, triumphal friezes, gilded ceilings and works of art.

Left *Paradise,* Tintoretto Centre **Wellhead** Right **Giants' Staircase**

Doge's Palace Art & Architecture

1 Paradise
Possibly the world's largest oil painting (1588–90), by Jacopo and Domenico Tintoretto, it is said to contain 800 figures (Sala del Maggior Consiglio).

2 Arcade Capital
Proclaimed the "most beautiful in Europe" by art critic John Ruskin, this eight-sided carved capital on the southwest corner shows the zodiac signs and planets in imaginative detail.

3 The Triumph of Venice
Dominating the Sala del Senato is Tintoretto's glorious work of propaganda (1580–84) showing allegorical and mythological figures proffering fruits of the sea to Venice.

4 Rape of Europe
Veronese's allegorical work (1580) in the Anticollegio shows Europe sitting on a bull, alias Jove, who is nuzzling her foot.

5 Drunkenness of Noah
A powerful sculpture from the early 1400s adorns the façade's southeast corner. Noah, inebriated and half-naked before his sons, is intended to portray the weakness of man.

6 Central Balcony
This magnificent early 15th-century stone terrace, embellished with columns, spires and a host of saints, opens off the Sala del Maggior Consiglio with a breathtaking view of the lagoon.

7 Giants' Staircase
So-named for its two colossal statues of Mars and Neptune, which were sculpted by Sansovino in 1567 as symbols of Venice's power. Visiting dignitaries would ascend the marble-lined stairs to the palace.

The Triumph of Venice, Tintoretto

8 Arco Foscari
This triumphal archway of pink-and-cream stone layers leading to the Giants' Staircase was commissioned by Doge Foscari in 1438.

9 Coronation of the Virgin
The faded but inspired remains of Guariento's fresco, discovered beneath Tintoretto's *Paradise,* are housed in a side room, with panels explaining the restoration techniques.

10 Wellheads
Elaborate 16th-century wellheads were constructed to drain water from the gutters to the central courtyard.

For more Venetian artists and architects **See pp44–5**

Top 10 Events in the Venetian Republic

The Extent of the Venetian Republic

In its earliest days, Venice was little more than a huddle of islands in the middle of a shallow marshy lagoon, settled by a band of refugees from the Veneto region. Yet over the centuries it developed into a mighty republic reaching south to the Mediterranean and north to the Alps, based on the concept of trade. Salt was stored in massive warehouses, there were dealings in exotic spices and wondrous fabrics from the East, crusades were organized and fitted out here and relics procured. Its main population probably never exceeded 160,000, however well beyond the walled port towns strung down the Dalmatian coast were far-flung outposts such as Crete and Cyprus. These dominions protected key passages in commerce with the Arabic countries. Westward across the Po plain, Venice's influence took in Treviso, Vicenza and Verona, extending all the way to Bergamo on the outskirts of Milan and the mighty Visconti dynasty.

A doctor during the Black Death

Marine Supremacy
The Republic's gaining of maritime power is celebrated in *The Victorious Return of Doge Andrea Contarini after Triumph in Chioggia* by Paolo Veronese (1525–88).

TOP 10 Piazza San Marco

Long the political and religious heart of Venice, it's hard to believe Piazza San Marco was once little more than a monastery garden crossed by a stream. The glittering basilica and Doge's Palace command the east side of the square, while other stately buildings along its borders have been the backdrop for magnificent processions celebrating victorious commanders, visiting dignitaries and festivals. The western end was remodelled by Napoleon, who wished to construct a royal palace here. Today the piazza continues to bustle, with a museum complex, elegant cafés, live orchestras, costumed Carnival crowds – not to mention duck-boards when it floods.

Campanile

Incomparable views of the city and lagoon can be had by taking the elevator to the top of this 98.5-m (323-ft) bell tower. Erstwhile lighthouse, watch tower and torture chamber, it was masterfully rebuilt to its 16th-century design following its clamorous collapse in 1902.

Bas-relief, *Doge's Palace* façade

🍷 An after-dinner drink in the piazza on summer evenings is accompanied by the café orchestras.

⏰ The best time to appreciate the beauty of the square is early morning, when only the city sweepers are here.

• San Marco
• Map Q5 • Campanile: Open Easter–Oct: 9am–7pm (9pm Jul & Aug), Nov–Easter: 9am–4:15pm (closed 2 weeks in Jan); admission €6.00
• Caffè Florian: 041 520 56 41: open 10am–midnight (closed Wed in winter)
• Museum Complex: Open Apr–Oct: 9am–7pm, Nov–Mar: 9am–5pm; admission €11

Top 10 Sights

1. Basilica San Marco
2. Doge's Palace
3. Torre dell'Orologio
4. Campanile
5. Piazzetta
6. Columns of San Marco & San Teodoro
7. Piazzetta dei Leoncini
8. Procuratie Vecchie & Nuove
9. Caffè Florian
10. Giardinetti Reali

Basilica San Marco
See pp8–11.

Doge's Palace
See pp12–15.

Torre dell'Orologio

A marvel to behold, the Renaissance-style clock tower features two bronze moors *(right)* hammering out the hours on the upper terrace. At Epiphany and Ascension there is an hourly procession of clockwork Magi led by an angel. According to legend, the craftsmen were blinded to prevent them repeating the work.

Plan of Piazza San Marco

Museo Correr

Librería Sansoviniana

Piazzetta
5 Once an inlet for boats and witness to the arrival of distinguished visitors during the Republic's heyday, this now fully paved mini square fronts the lagoon.

Caffè Florian
9 Reputedly Europe's first coffee house *(below)*, the premises still retain their 1720 wood-panelling, marble-topped tables and gilt-framed mirrors *(see p75)*.

Giardinetti Reali
10 These shady public gardens, created during the Napoleonic era, took the place of boatyards and grain stores, situated just behind the panoramic waterfront.

Venice's Bells

Booming through the city, the five bells in the Campanile have marked Venice's rhythms for centuries. The Maleficio bell announced an execution, the Nona rang at midday, the Trottiera spurred on the nobles' horses for assemblies in the Doge's Palace and the Mezza Terza marked a session of the Senate. The Marangona still tolls at midnight.

Columns of San Marco and San Teodoro
6 These two granite columns *(right)* with symbols of the saints were erected in 1172 by Nicolò Barattieri. Public executions were held here.

Piazzetta dei Leoncini
7 Site of a former vegetable market, a pair of lions *(leoni)* in red Verona stone have been crouching here since 1722.

Procuratie Vecchie and Nuove
8 These elegant 15th-century buildings were the residence of the Procurators, responsible for state administration.

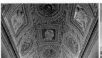 

Left **Libreria Sansoviniana staircase ceiling** Centre **Bellini Room** Right **Correr Ballroom**

Museo Correr Complex

1 Biblioteca Marciana Ceiling
The ceiling vault of the opulent reading room (sale monumentali), inside the Libreria Sansoviniana, collapsed in 1545 and its architect Sansovino imprisoned – he was released to complete the job at his own expense. Titian selected artists for the decorations; Veronese was awarded a gold chain for the best work.

2 Libreria Sansoviniana Staircase
Bedecked with gilt and stucco decorations by Alessandro Vittoria, the 16th-century staircase leads from a monumental entrance on the piazza to the halls of the old library.

3 Veneziano Paintings
This prolific Byzantine artist is featured in the Pinacoteca's Room 25 (part of Museo Correr), with glowing two-dimensional religious portraits (1290–1302).

4 Correr Ballroom
This showy Neo-Classical creation was built for Napoleon. It is now used for exhibitions.

5 Two Venetian Ladies
Carpaccio's masterpiece of well-dressed ladies (1500–10) is in Room 38 of the Museo Correr. First thought to depict courtesans, the women are, in fact, awaiting their menfolk's return from hunting.

6 Map of Venice
Pride of place in Room 32 of the Museo Correr goes to Jacopo de' Barbari's prospective map-layout of Venice (1497–1500), painstakingly engraved on six pear-wood panels.

7 Bellini Room
Works by the talented Bellini family are on display in Room 36 of the Pinacoteca: the poignant *Dead Christ Supported by Two Angels* (1453–5) by the best known, Giovanni; head of the family, Jacopo's *Crucifixion* (1450) and son Gentile's portrait of *Doge Giovanni Mocenigo* (1475).

8 Canova Statues
Foremost sculptor of his time, works by Antonio Canova (1767–1822) in the Museo Correr include his acclaimed statue *Daedalus and Icarus*.

9 Narwhal Tusk
Once prized as the horn of the fabled unicorn, this 1.6-m-long (5-ft) tusk from the rare whale has been superbly carved with Jesse's and Jesus's family tree (Room 40 in Museo Correr).

10 Crafts & Guilds
Wooden sandals 60 cm (2 ft) high, inlaid with mother-of-pearl, illustrate the stiff demands of 15th–17th-century fashions (Room 48).

Venus statue, Canova

The complex on San Marco includes Museo Correr, Libreria Sansoviniana and the Archeological Museum

Top 10 Historic Events in Piazza San Marco

1. Foundations of Doge's Palace laid (AD 814)
2. Construction of basilica started (828)
3. First bullfight held (1162)
4. Square paved with brick, herringbone-style (1267)
5. Square paved with volcanic trachyte blocks (1722–35)
6. Napoleon demolishes San Geminiano church to make way for Ala Napoleonica (1810)
7. Campanile crumbles to the ground (1902)
8. Record flood 1.94 m (6.4 ft) above sea level (4 November 1966)
9. Pink Floyd rock concert attracts 100,000 (1989)
10. Campanile stormed by separatists (1997)

Acqua Alta Flooding

Acqua Alta ("high water") has long been disruptive to the city between October and March. As warning sirens fill the air, people drag out their waterproof boots, shopkeepers rush to put up protective barriers and street-sweepers lay out duck-boards in low-lying spots. Venice and its lagoon are subject to the tides of the Adriatic Sea but flood levels are caused by the coincidence of low atmospheric pressure, strong sirocco winds from the south and natural high tides due to moon phases. Piazza San Marco is among the most vulnerable spots. The flood gates designed for the Lido sea entrances are held by many experts to be both useless and harmful to the lagoon, however there are plans for an elaborate drainage system on the piazza, dredging canals and raising paving levels.

The Acqua Alta
Being in a vulnerable position on the edge of the lagoon, Piazza San Marco has been flooded by high tides throughout its history.

Piazza San Marco's worst floods, November 1966

19

🔟 Grand Canal

Venice's majestic "highway", the Canal Grande, is only one of the 177 canals flowing through the city, but at some 4 km (2.5 miles) in length, 30–70 m (98–230 ft) in width and averaging 4.5 m (15 ft) in depth, it certainly earns its name. Snaking its way through the city with a double curve, its banks are lined with exquisite palaces, while on its waters colourful flotillas of gondolas, ferries, taxi launches, high-speed police boats and barges groaning under loads of fresh produce, provide endless fascination. In 1818, when the water was cleaner, Lord Byron swam all the way down the Grand Canal from the Lido.

Top 10 Sights

1. Fondaco dei Turchi
2. Ca' Pesaro
3. Rialto Bridge
4. Riva del Vin
5. Ca' Rezzonico
6. Accademia Bridge
7. Ca' Dario
8. Santa Maria delle Salute
9. Punta della Dogana
10. Harry's Bar

Fondaco dei Turchi façade

🡆 Grab the front seats on *vaporetto* line No. 1 for the trip of a lifetime.

To beat the crowds, either start out from Piazzale Roma heading towards San Marco late afternoon or evening, or take the reverse direction in the morning.

• *The Grand Canal runs from Piazzale Roma, the bus terminal and car park area, to Piazza San Marco. It is navigable courtesy of ferries Nos. 1 (all stops) and 82 (main stops only).*

1 Fondaco dei Turchi

With an exotic air and distinctive round arches, this Veneto-Byzantine building (1225) was the Turkish trade centre for 200 years. It is now the Natural History Museum *(see p64)*.

2 Ca' Pesaro

This colossal Baroque palace, decorated with diamond-point ashlar work, was the final creation of architect Longhena. Home to the city's modern art collections, it is beautifully floodlit at night *(see p41)*.

3 Rialto Bridge

One of the city's most familiar views, the striking 28-m (92-ft) span, 8-m (26-ft) high Istrian stone Ponte di Rialto *(below)* dates from 1588.

For more Venice bridges See pp46–7

Riva del Vin
A sunny quayside with a string of open-air restaurants, this is one of the few accessible banks of the Grand Canal. Barrels of wine *(vino)* used to be off-loaded here, hence the name.

Ca' Rezzonico
The finest feature of this imposing palace is its grandiose staircase. Today it is a museum of 18th-century Venice.

Accademia Bridge
The lovely wooden Ponte dell'Accademia, built in 1932 by the engineer Miozzi, was intended as a temporary measure until a more substantial structure was designed, but it is now a permanent fixture. It affords stunning views of the Grand Canal.

Wave-induced Damage

Damage to buildings caused by wash has worsened of late with the spiralling increase of motor-propelled craft. Waves provoked by all manner of boats eat into foundations of buildings set on the water's edge, as well as making life harder for the gondoliers. Speed limits aim to curb this: 7 kmph (4.5 mph) for private craft and 11 kmph (7 mph) for public waterbuses on the Grand Canal. Narrower canals mean 5 kmph (3 mph), whereas 20 kmph (12.5 mph) is the maximum on the lagoon.

Ca' Dario
With an ornamental Renaissance façade studded with multicoloured stone medallions, this lopsided palace is supposedly cursed due to a number of misfortunes that have overtaken its various owners.

Santa Maria della Salute
Longhena's 17th-century masterpiece of sculpted whorls beneath a towering dome, this church commemorates the end of a devastating plague in the city (see p38).

Punta della Dogana
The figure of Fortune stands atop the erstwhile customs house, doubling as a weather vane. This is where the Grand Canal joins St Mark's Basin and the lagoon.

Harry's Bar
Legendary watering hole of Ernest Hemingway, this is also where the Bellini apéritif was invented (see p57). Opened in 1931 by Arrigo Cipriani, it was named after the American who funded the enterprise.

Stonework damaged by waves

Left *Traghetto* on the Grand Canal Centre *Vaporetto* stop Right *Motonave* on the lagoon

🔟 Watercraft of Venice

1 Gondola
Most commonly seen transporting tourists, a larger version is also used for the cross-canal ferry *(see p135)*, while the smaller *gondolino* is a slender racing craft.

2 Vaporetto
Strictly speaking, this is the capacious rounded waterbus, now also seen in an "ecological" electric model. A slimmer *motoscafo* serves the outer runs and narrow canals with relatively low bridges.

Vaporetto

3 Sandolo
A slim lightweight boat perfectly suited to hunting and fishing in the shallow waters of the lagoon, not to mention racing. Painted black, these "imitation gondolas" can deceive tourists on the back canals.

4 Topo
The most common barge for transporting goods, it can be seen loaded with everything from washing machines to demi-johns, often with a live dog "figurehead" on the prow.

5 Sanpierota
This flat-bottomed rowing boat is named after the inhabitants of San Pietro in Volta in the southern lagoon *(see p117)*. Once used for transporting fish to Venice, nowadays it is fitted with an outboard motor and photogenic oblique sail.

6 Bragozzo
With a gently rounded prow and stern, this brightly coloured sailing boat was traditionally used for fishing by the inhabitants of Chioggia *(see p117)*.

7 Fire Boat
From their station near Ca' Foscari, the red launches are called both to deal with fires and to rescue submerged obstacles and crumbling façades.

8 Garbage Vessel
The city's hefty waste-collecting AMAV barges trundle over the lagoon with the day's rubbish, as well as carrying out environmental monitoring.

9 Ambulance and Police Launches
These modern craft attract plenty of attention as they roar down the canals – only the emergency categories are allowed to disregard the city's speed limits.

10 Car Ferry
These brand new giants convey all manner of motor vehicles from the Tronchetto to the Lido.

For more on getting around Venice **See p135**

Top 10 Gondola Features

1. *Forcola* (rowlock)
2. *Ferro* (prow bracket)
3. *Hippocampus* (side ornament)
4. Night lamp
5. Bronze stern decoration
6. Ribbed oar
7. *Felze* (cabin)
8. Gondolier's foot rest
9. Gondolier's striped shirt
10. Gondolier's straw hat

Venice's Gondolas

The quintessential sleek Venetian gondola has been plying the city's canals since as early as the 11th century, although it did not take on its present graceful form until the late 1400s. Compared to a mere 405 gondolas on the waterways today, as many as 10,000 were in use in the late 19th century: bridges were once few and far between and gondolas acted as ferries between one island and another, a custom that continues to this day across the Grand Canal.

Gondolier in traditional dress

A handful of gondola yards still construct the boats as well as carrying out repairs, such as San Trovaso in Dorsoduro (see p89). It's a costly and complex craft – eight different types of wood are needed for a total of 280 pieces to put together the asymmetrical craft, 11 m (36 ft) in length and 1.42 m (4.5 ft) in width, at a cost approaching 25,000 euros. A gondola weighs more than 350 kg (770 lb), including a 30-kg (66-lb) ferro (iron bracket) on the prow, to offset the weight of the rower. Originally painted in bright colours, the black gondolas that you see today were decreed by the Senate to prevent excessive shows of wealth.

Gondola mooring post

La Sensa Festival *(see p62)*

23

🔟 Accademia Galleries

A dazzling collection of masterpieces spanning the full development of Venetian art from Byzantine to Renaissance, Baroque and Rococo, the Gallerie dell'Accademia is Venice's equivalent of the Uffizi in Florence. Giovanni Battista Piazzetta started the collection in 1750 to serve as models for the art school; in 1807 it was boosted by Napoleon with the addition of works from suppressed churches. The same year the collection moved to its present premises, occupying three former religious establishments: the 12th–15th-century Scuola Grande di Santa Maria della Carità and its adjoining church, and a 12th-century monastery remodelled by Palladio in the 1500s. More recently, in the 1940s, Carlo Scarpa modernized the layout (see p45).

The Tempest
This enigmatic 1506 portrayal of a woman suckling her child is by Giorgione (Room 5). The overall impression is of figures and the dream-like, stormy landscape blended into one whole.

Accademia Galleries entrance

❥ Read the helpful free information sheets available in each room. They contain almost entirely the same text as the audio guide.

Top 10 Works

1. San Giobbe Altarpiece
2. The Tempest
3. Supper in the House of Levi
4. Pietà
5. Meeting and Departure of the Betrothed Ursula and Ereo
6. Procession in St Mark's Square
7. Madonna dell'Arancio
8. Coronation of the Virgin
9. Portrait of a Gentleman
10. Portraits by Rosalba Carriera

• *Campo della Carità Dorsoduro 1050*
• *Map L6*
• *041 522 22 47*
• *Open 8:15am–7:15pm daily (2pm Mon; last admission 30 minutes before closing); closed 1 Jan, 1 May, 25 Dec*
• *Admission €6.50*
• *Quadreria Corridor: 041 522 22 47 (reservations essential); opening times vary, phone to check; tours in Italian only, free of charge*
• *Bookshop • www.gallerieaccademia.org*

San Giobbe Altarpiece
Giovanni Bellini's gloriously inspirational altarpiece (Room 2), was painted in 1487 for the Church of San Giobbe. It is regarded as one of the finest examples of *Sacra Conversazione*, which was central to 15th-century Venetian art. The presence of St Sebastian and St Roch alongside the Virgin suggest the aftermath of plague, while angel musicians pay homage to San Giobbe, patron saint of music.

For more Venice museums and galleries **See pp40–41**

Supper in the House of Levi

The forceful canvas by Veronese (1573) occupies an entire wall of Room 10 *(below)* and caused controversy in its time. The church authorities, who commissioned it as "The Last Supper", were angered by the inclusion of "dogs, buffoons, drunken Germans, dwarfs and other such absurdities" – so Veronese changed the title.

Pietà

Titian's last work (1576) is unfinished but it is also considered his best (Room 10), imbued as it is with golden light and a piercing sense of anguish.

Meeting and Departure of the Betrothed Ursula and Ereo

Part of Carpaccio's magnificent narrative cycle (1495) about a Breton princess and an English prince can be seen in Room 21.

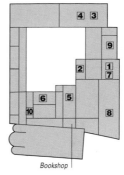

Bookshop

Gallery Floorplan

Portraits by Rosalba Carriera

As a female artist in demand by 18th-century high society, Carriera *(self-portrait below)* was a rarity for her time. Her late-Baroque works in Room 17 display the soft romantic pastels that became her trademark.

Procession in St Mark's Square

Part of Gentile Bellini's spectacular cycle (1496) of the St Mark's Day procession in 1444 is seen in Room 20.

La Madonna dell'Arancio

This exquisite work (1496–8) by Cima da Conegliano, painted for a Murano Franciscan church, is enlivened with partridges and plant life (Room 2).

Coronation of the Virgin

This resplendent polyptych (1350) by Venice's leading 14th-century artist, Paolo Veneziano, is the first work in Room 1. Flanking the sumptuous Byzantine-inspired centre are events from the life of Christ.

Portrait of a Gentleman

Lorenzo Lotto's sombre image of a melancholic man of means in his study (1528) is possibly a self portrait (Room 7). Lotto was known for work entailing psychological insights.

Gallery Guide

The vast gallery is organized in chronological order for the most part and the 24 rooms, labelled with roman numerals, are equipped with explanatory cards in English. The Quadreria corridor, a former storage area, is filled with masterpieces. Reached via a fine free-standing spiral staircase by Andrea Palladio, it is visited free of charge.

For more on Venice artists **See p44**

25

TOP 10 Santa Maria Gloriosa dei Frari

A masterpiece of Venetian Gothic ecclesiastical architecture, this cavernous 15th-century church for Franciscan friars took more than 100 years to complete, along with its "brother" SS Giovanni e Paolo (see p38), and a further 26 years for the consecration of the main altar. A wonderful series of art treasures is held within the deceptively gloomy interior, which is almost 100 m (330 ft) long and 50 m (165 ft) across, from priceless canvases by Titian and Bellini to tombs of doges and artists such as Canova.

Titian's monument

🍽 There are some great cafés and eateries in Campo dei Frari with views of the church.

👦 Youngsters will love the nativity scene with day-night lighting effects and moving figures at Christmas time.

• Campo dei Frari, San Polo
• Map L3
• 041 275 04 62
• Open 9am–6pm Mon–Sat, 1–6pm Sun; closed 1 Jan, Easter, 15 Aug, 25 Dec
• Admission €2.50

Top 10 Features

1. Assumption of the Virgin
2. Rood Screen
3. Choir Stalls
4. Madonna Enthroned with Saints
5. Campanile
6. Canova's Mausoleum
7. Monument to Doge Francesco Foscari
8. Statue of John the Baptist
9. Monument to Titian
10. Mausoleum of Doge Giovanni Pesaro

1 Assumption of the Virgin

Titian's glowing 1518 depiction of the triumphant ascent of Mary shows her robed in crimson accompanied by a semi-circle of saints, while the 12 Apostles are left gesticulating in wonderment below. This brilliant canvas on the high altar is the inevitable focus of the church.

2 Rood Screen

A beautifully carved blend of Renaissance and Gothic elements by Pietro Lombardo and Bartolomeo Bon (1475), the screen divides the worship area and nave *(below)*.

3 Choir Stalls

Unique for Venice, the original three tiers of 124 friars' seats deserve examination for their fascinating inlaid woodwork. Crafted by Marco Cozzi in 1468, they show the influence of northern European styles.

For more Venice churches **See pp38–9**

4 Madonna Enthroned with Saints

Tucked away in the sacristy, and still in its original engraved frame, is another delight for Bellini fans (1488). "It seems painted with molten gems," wrote Henry James of the triptych.

5 Campanile

The robust 14th-century bell tower set into the church's left transept is the second tallest in Venice.

Church Floorplan

6 Canova's Mausoleum

This colossal monument, based on Canova's Neo-Classical design for Titian's tomb, which was never built, was a tribute by the sculptor's followers in 1822.

7 Monument to Doge Francesco Foscari

A fine Renaissance tribute to the man responsible for Venice's mainland expansion. Foscari was the subject of Lord Byron's *The Two Foscari,* turned into an opera by Verdi.

8 Statue of John the Baptist

The inspirational wood statue from 1450 *(left),* created especially for the church by artist Donatello (1386–1466), stands in the Florentine chapel. The emaciated figure is particularly lifelike.

9 Monument to Titian

Titian was afforded special authorization for burial here after his death during the 1576 plague, although this sturdy mausoleum was not built for another 300 years.

10 Mausoleum of Doge Giovanni Pesaro

The monsters and black marble figures supporting the sarcophagus of this macabre Baroque monument prompted art critic John Ruskin to write "it seems impossible for false taste and base feeling to sink lower".

State Archives

The labyrinthine monastery and courtyards adjoining the church have been home to Venice's State Archives since the fall of the Republic. Its 300 rooms and approximately 70 km (43 miles) of shelves are loaded with precious records documenting the history of Venice right back to the 9th century, including the Golden Book register of the Venetian aristocracy. Scholars enter the building via the Oratorio di San Nicolò della Lattuga (1332), named after the miraculous recovery of a Procurator of San Marco thanks to the healing qualities of a lettuce *(lattuga).*

TOP10 Rialto Market

The commercial hub of Venice is as bustling today as it has always been – records tell of markets here since 1097. The area is also the city's historical heart and took its name from Rivoaltus, the high consolidated terrain that guaranteed early settlers flood-free premises. The majority of buildings, however, date from the 16th century, due to a fire which swept through Rialto in 1514. During Carnival the stall-holders don medieval costume to vie with each other for custom and only the new awnings and electronic cash registers let slip the modern world.

Fabbriche Nuove arcades

🍴 In addition to fresh fruit from the market, picnic supplies can be bought at the delicatessens and bakeries in the neighbourhood.

- San Polo
- Map P2
- Fresh produce market: 7:30am–1pm Mon–Sat; Pescheria: 7:30am–1pm Tue–Sat

1 Fresh Produce Market
A treat for the senses, with artistic piles of luscious peaches and cherries, thorny artichokes and red chicory from Treviso. Fruit, vegetables and fish tend to be strictly seasonal.

2 Pescheria
Writhing eels, soft-shelled crabs, huge swordfish and crimson-fleshed fresh tuna are among the stars of the 1907 Neo-Gothic fish market hall *(above)*, barely out of reach of the scavenging, screeching seagulls.

3 San Giacomo di Rialto
The oldest church in Venice claims to have a foundation set by a pious carpenter in the 5th century, although the present building is medieval. The Gothic portico and 24-hour clock are well worth a look.

For more on shopping in Venice **See p138**

Public Rostrum
New laws and names of criminals were announced atop this porphyry column, supported by a stone figure known as *il gobbo* (hunchback).

Palazzo dei Camerlenghi
This lop-sided 1525 palace *(right)* once imprisoned debtors on the ground floor, but the top floors were offices for the city treasurers *(camerlenghi)*.

Gondola Ferry
A must for every visitor is a trip on the *traghetto* ferry across the Grand Canal – one of only eight still in operation. Custom dictates that passengers should remain standing.

Banco Giro Arcade
Merchants gathered to do business deals outside the city's first bank set up in 1157, now a wine bar. The state abolished private institutions in 1585, profiting from the activity.

Ruga degli Orefici
This lovely covered passageway decorated with frescoes has been home to silversmiths, goldsmiths and silk traders since the 1300s.

Fabbriche Nuove
Uniformed *carabinieri* (police) patrol the elongated law courts edging the Grand Canal *(below)*. Designed in 1552–5 by Sansovino they are recognizable by their 25 plain arcades.

Grand Canal Views
The Erberia, right on the Grand Canal, makes a wonderful spot for boat-watching since the relocation of the wholesale market from here to Tronchetto in the 1990s.

CAMPO DE LA PESCARIA

Place Names
Rialto market's narrow alleyways carry names such as Orefici (goldsmiths), Pescaria (fishmongers) and Erberia (vegetables), because the same type of shops once stood together. Local eateries for market traders also had evocative names such as Scimia (Monkey) and Do Mori (Two Moors).

🔟 Torcello

Some of the most breathtaking Byzantine mosaics in the world, found in the lagoon's oldest building, the Torcello basilica, reward those who visit this laid-back island, a beautiful 60-minute ferry ride from northern Venice. From the 5th century, mainlanders fleeing invading Lombards and Huns ventured across tidal flats to found a settlement that grew to 20,000 and lasted 1,000 years. However few clues to the past remain, as the canals silted up, malaria decimated the population and the power base shifted to Venice once and for all. Today Torcello is home to a handful of gardeners and fishermen.

Santa Fosca façade

⊘ Insect repellent is a must in summer as fierce mosquitoes have colonized the open lagoon.

• Boat line LN from the Fondamente Nuove via Murano and Burano or from San Marco via Lido
• Map H1
• Basilica di Santa Maria dell'Assunta; 041 296 0630; open Mar–Oct: 10:30am–6pm daily, Nov–Feb: 10am–5pm daily; admission €3.00
• Campanile: open Mar–Oct: 10:30am–5:30pm daily, Nov–Feb: 10am–5pm; admission €3.00; audio guide.
• Santa Fosca: open for worship only.
• Museo dell'Estuario: 041 730 761; open Mar–Oct: 10:30am–5:30pm Tue–Sun, Nov–Feb: 10am–5pm Tue–Sun; closed public hols; admission €3.00.

Top 10 Sights

1. Basilica Exterior
2. Doomsday Mosaics
3. Apse Mosaics
4. Iconostasis
5. Paving
6. Campanile
7. Throne of Attila
8. Museo dell'Estuario
9. Santa Fosca
10. Locanda Cipriani

1 Basilica Exterior
A miraculous survivor, this striking cathedral was founded in 639 but underwent radical restructuring in 1008. It retains its Romanesque form, light brick walls and an arcaded 9th-century portico.

2 Doomsday Mosaics, Basilica
In these 12–13th-century marvels *(below)* the *Universal Judgment* is dramatically depicted in superbly restored scenes of devils, angels, wild beasts and fires.

3 Apse Mosaics, Basilica
This moving 13th-century mosaic shows the Virgin in a blue robe with gold fringing, cradling her radiant child in a gentle stance. Below are the 12 Apostles standing in a meadow of flowers.

4 Iconostasis, Basilica
Exquisite marble panels show peacocks drinking at the fountain of eternal life, diminutive lions posing under a tree of tendrils loaded with birds, while six columns support 15th-century paintings of the Apostles with the Virgin.

For more on the Northern Lagoon islands **See pp108–13**

5 Paving, Basilica

In vivid swirls of colours, rivalling the flooring in Basilica San Marco, are brilliant 11th-century *tesserae* of stone and glass. Cubes, semi-circles and triangles are laid into square designs. The floor level was raised 30 cm (1 ft) during the basilica's reconstruction.

8 Museo dell'Estuario

An intriguing if modest collection of archaeological finds from the island and priceless treasures from the church, are housed in adjoining Gothic buildings *(above)*.

Attila the Hun

The "Scourge of God", otherwise known as the King of the Huns, ruled from AD 434–53 with an empire stretching from the Alps and the Baltic towards the Caspian Sea. As part of his campaign against the Roman Empire, Attila attacked the cities of Milan, Verona and Padua causing refugees to flee to Torcello. Burning the cathedral town of Aquileia gave him special satisfaction – his men raised a hill in Udine so he could enjoy the spectacle.

6 Campanile

The views from this simple 55-m (180-ft) bell tower range over the vast expanse of the lagoon, with its meandering canals and tidal flats, to the Adriatic Sea, Venice itself and even north to the Alps on a clear winter's day.

9 Santa Fosca

Alongside the basilica is this elegant church based on a Greek cross design, encircled by a five-sided portico with columns and carved capitals. The inside of the church is usually closed at lunchtime.

7 Throne of Attila

By popular belief this marble armchair *(right)* was the throne of the king of the Huns, though historical sources claim it was for the island's magistrates.

10 Locanda Cipriani

A favourite of Ernest Hemingway, who stayed here in 1948, the quiet charm of this guesthouse has attracted VIPs since it opened in 1938 (see p146).

Attila, barbaric King of the Huns

Campo Santa Margherita

This cheery, picturesque square in the district of Dorsoduro is a hive of activity day in, day out. It owes its name to the Christian martyr St Margaret of Antioch, possibly a fictitious figure but highly popular in medieval times. Patron saint of expectant mothers, she is depicted in a niche on the square's northern wall with her emblem, the dragon. The square's capacious form, exploited by local children on bicycles and in-line skates, is due to an ambitious enlargement project in the 1800s which opened up the south end by filling in canals.

Chiesa dei Carmini façade

Top 10 Sights

1. Ex Chiesa di Santa Margherita
2. Palazzo Foscolo-Corner
3. Scuola Grande dei Carmini
4. Calle del Forno
5. Casa dei Varoteri
6. Corte del Fondaco
7. Chiesa di Santa Maria dei Carmini
8. The "House of the Moor"
9. Rio Novo
10. Altana Terraces

🍴 Numerous take-away pizza slice outlets and bars serving sandwiches *(tramezzini)* and rolls *(panini)* make for a cheap lunch, and allow for the kids to run around.

• Dorsoduro
• Map K5
• Scuola Grande dei Carmini: 041 528 9420; open Apr–Oct: 9am–6pm Mon–Sat, 9am–4pm Sun; Nov–Mar: 9am–4pm daily; admission €5.00.

1 Ex Chiesa di Santa Margherita
A writhing 14th-century dragon symbolizing the martyrdom of the saint enlivens the foot of the bell tower of the former church. It has been restored by the university as the Auditorium Santa Margherita.

2 Palazzo Foscolo-Corner
This beautiful palace *(below)* is virtually unchanged since the 1300s and instantly distinguishable by its deep overhanging eaves. A striking Byzantine-style lunette, bearing an inset with the family crest, tops the entrance portal.

3 Scuola Grande dei Carmini
Glorious rooms decorated with Tiepolo's masterpieces are highlights of this confraternity. The upstairs ceiling shows *St Simeon Stock Receiving the Scapular from the Virgin.*

For more on Venice's Dorsoduro district **See pp88–93**

4 Calle del Forno
An unusual series of medieval-style projections from a first-floor dwelling, partly held up by brick columns, is one of the features of this busy thoroughfare leading to Piazzale Roma and the bus terminal. The street is named after a long-gone bakery *(forno)*.

5 Casa dei Varoteri
A splendid *bas-relief* of the Virgin sheltering a group of tradesmen in adoration adorns the former tanners' guild dating from 1725. Because of its isolated position, it was once mistakenly thought to be the house of the city's executioner.

Rio Terrà dei Catecumeni, Dorsoduro

Rio Terrà
Rio is a common name for canal, while *terrà* means filled-in. Dating back to the 14th century, the practice of filling in waterways was particularly widespread in the 1800s to provide extra pedestrian space. Some would be covered over with a system of low-slung arches so as not to obstruct water flow, exemplified by Via Garibaldi in Castello *(see p102)*. Recent campaigns, however, have encouraged the reverse procedure, with Cannaregio's Rio della Crea re-opened.

6 Corte del Fondaco
A charming covered passageway leads through to this minor courtyard where curious low bricked-in arches indicate the former site of a 1700s flour store. The name *fondaco* or store derived from the Arabic *fonduq*.

7 Chiesa di Santa Maria dei Carmini
This richly adorned church happily survived Napoleon's suppression of the Carmelite order of monks in the adjoining monastery. Many of its 13th-century features are intact, such as the sculpted entrance porch.

8 The "House of the Moor"
Research has proved that Shakespeare's *Othello* was based on Cristoforo Moro, son of a noble family sent to govern the island of Cyprus from 1508. This house at No. 2615 is his former home.

9 Rio Novo
Excavated in 1932–3 to form a short cut from Piazzale Roma to the Grand Canal, the canal *(right)* has been closed to *vaporetti* since the 1990s, due to building damage.

10 Altana Terraces
These timber roof platforms were common in Venetian palaces and used by the ladies of the house for bleaching their hair, which they exposed to the sun through a crownless wide-brimmed hat. They are now used for washing and drying clothes, and partying on balmy summer evenings.

Peggy Guggenheim Collection

The delightfully spacious, light-filled Collezione Peggy Guggenheim is home to works by more than 200 contemporary artists representing powerful avant garde movements such as Cubism, Futurism and Surrealism. The landmark collection, put together by its far-sighted namesake, is housed in the 18th-century Palazzo Venier dei Leoni, known as the "unfinished palace" because of its one-storey construction. As well as the wonderful works of art on display inside the gallery, there is also a striking sculpture garden and the former home of Peggy Guggenheim to visit.

2 Bird in Space

This polished brass sculpture (1932–40) was once classified by US customs as a "stair-rail", thus subject to duty. Its creator was Romanian artist Constantin Brancusi (1876–1957).

Palazzo Venier dei Leoni façade

🍴 Take a break on the café's shady verandah for a light snack or a meal.

🌅 Watch the sun setting on the terrace directly on the Grand Canal during the late evening openings.

Fondamenta Venier dei Leoni, Dorsoduro 704 (2nd entrance Calle S Cristoforo, Dorsoduro 701)
• Map D5
• 041 240 54 11
• www.guggenheim-venice.it
• Open 10am–6pm Wed–Mon; closed 25 Dec
• Admission €10
• Coffee shop
• Audio guides
• No photography
• Shop

Top 10 Works of Art

1 The Poet
2 Bird in Space
3 Attirement of the Bride
4 Empire of Light
5 Woman Walking
6 The Moon Woman
7 Magic Garden
8 Mobile
9 Angel of the City
10 Three Standing Figures

1 The Poet

A wonderful starting point is this portrait (1911) by legendary Spanish artist Pablo Picasso (1881–1973), from his early Cubist period. The figure is executed from a limited palette of ochre and dark browns *(below)*.

3 Attirement of the Bride

This portrayal (1940) of an orange-robed bride assisted by mutant animals and humans *(above)*, is by Max Ernst (1891–1976). The German Surrealist was married to Guggenheim in the 1940s.

For more Venice art galleries **See pp40–41**

4 Empire of Light
Magical light effects see darkened trees and a house silhouetted by a street lamp against a contrasting daytime sky with fluffy clouds, in this work (1953–4) by René Magritte (1898–1967). The Belgian Surrealist was renowned for his eccentric subjects.

5 Woman Walking
This serene elongated form of a truncated female figure (1932), apparently inspired by Etruscan design, is the recognized trademark of the Swiss artist Alberto Giacometti (1901–66), a short-term participant in the Surrealist movement.

Terrace

Gianni Mattioli Collection

Main entrance

Key to floorplan
- Gallery
- Nasher Sculpture Garden

7 Magic Garden
A deliberately child-like, warmly textured piece (1926) by Paul Klee (1879–1940), with smeary shapes and sketched-in faces and buildings *(below)*, fulfils the artist's desire to be "as though newborn... to be almost primitive".

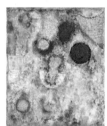

8 Mobile
This simple master-piece of movement (1941) by Alexander Calder (1898–1976), which gave its name to all mobiles, hangs in the atrium of Guggenheim's house and shifts delicately in the breeze.

10 Three Standing Figures
Beautifully placed in the Nasher Sculpture Garden, these abstract sculptures (1953) by Henry Moore (1898–1986) were inspired by Italian bell towers.

Peggy Guggenheim
This colourful US expatriate (1898–1979) and heir to a mining fortune first came to Europe in 1921, quickly fitting into Bohemian Paris. Resolving to "buy a picture a day", she amassed a contemporary art collection which was exhibited in both London and New York, before she made Venice her home in 1947. She is fondly remembered by locals for her faithful dogs and for owning the city's last private gondola.

6 The Moon Woman
This vibrant canvas (1942) starring a skeletal stick figure with an odd, padded curve is an early work by Jackson Pollock (1912–56), pre-dating his famous "drip" technique.

9 Angel of the City
Set on steps leading to the terrace, this bronze horse and rider (1948) by Italian sculptor Marino Marini (1901–80) greet passing boats in an outstretched stance.

Guggenheim and dogs

Left **Getting around on the water** Right **Crumbling Venetian façade**

🔟 Frequently Asked Questions

1 Is Venice still sinking?

Theoretically, that all came to a halt when the industries in Marghera stopped pumping out groundwater. However, recent studies document both a rise in relative sea level, combined with accelerating subsidence due to changes in plate tectonics and soft sediments compacting under the weight of buildings.

2 What do the buildings stand on?

In the course of the city's history, millions of pinewood piles from the Republic's carefully cultivated forests in the Alps were driven deep into the compressed clay-mud base and, over time, petrified in the absence of oxygen. These were successively overlaid with horizontal planks and marble-like Istrian stone slabs which served as the foundations for buildings.

Venetian brick façade

3 Do people often fall in the water?

The odd tourist miscalculates the distance between the quayside and a waiting water taxi and takes the plunge – inevitably saved by timely intervention from a bystander. Be wary of moss-covered steps when taking a photograph or a rest and, of course, don't let young children out of your sight near water.

4 Why don't people restore the crumbling buildings?

Strict regulations concern façades – only porous stucco can be used for renovation as anything else tends to come away in sheets in damp, windy weather and is a hazard for passers-by. As a result, freshly plastered façades start crumbling weeks after application due to the high humidity and salt content in the air.

5 How deep is the lagoon?

At its maximum, 15 m (49 ft) in the navigable channels dredged for shipping and marked by bricole poles. Concern about the danger of silting and obstruction of the city's lifeline waterways has always been high – one preventitive measure was to re-route two rivers into the Adriatic Sea away from the lagoon. The Brenta was gradually modified between 1400–1600 to have it flow out after Chioggia, and the Sile was redirected towards Jesolo in the 1600s.

6 Does everyone have a boat?

On summer Sundays you would be forgiven for thinking that is the case, as families pack small craft with picnic supplies, sunshades, fishing or stereo gear and row, sail, punt or speed out across the lagoon. Many, of course, need boats for work. On average, one in two families possess a pleasure boat.

Private pleasure boats belonging to Venice residents

7 How many people actually live in Venice?

The 1997 census states 68,600, meaning figures have more than halved since the 1950s. Moreover, this includes Italy's highest percentage of senior citizens. Venice's permanent population is experiencing a slow but inexorable decline as young couples prefer to move to the mainland with the convenience of a car, not to mention lower house prices, cheaper shopping and fewer tourists.

8 Can you drink water from the drinking fountains?

Yes, it's the same as the tap water and subject to constant testing and treatment. Until 1884, when the supply piped from the mainland was inaugurated with a fountain in Piazza San Marco, the city depended on rainwater which was meticulously drained and collected in cisterns beneath squares equipped with locked covered wells.

Drinking fountain

9 How does the house numbering system work?

Within each of the city's six administrative districts (*sestiere*), numbers follow the alleyways along one side at a time, taking in branch streets and courtyards when encountered. In Cannaregio, the most extensive district, numbers reach 6420. The postmen are used to this confusing system, but visitors will need the name of the alley (*calle*), square (*campo*) or quayside (*fondamenta*).

Venice house number

10 Is the sea safe for swimming?

Yes. Periodic controls for bacterial counts are carried out and the upper Adriatic normally emerges with a clean slate. Venice's closest beach is at the Lido, where the city's families go en masse during the steamy summer months (see p115).

Left & centre left **S Maria G dei Frari** Centre right **Madonna dell'Orto** Right **S Maria dei Miracoli**

🔟 Venice Churches

Basilica San Marco
See *pp8–11*.

Santa Maria Gloriosa dei Frari
See *pp26–7*.

Santi Giovanni e Paolo
The monumental tombs of 25 doges take pride of place in this solemn Gothic giant, erected by Dominican friars from the 13th to 15th centuries. Among them is the grandiose tribute to Pietro Mocenigo for his valorous struggle to defend Venice's eastern colonies against the Turks (west wall). Inside are splendid paintings by Veronese and a polyptych (1465) by Giovanni Bellini.
🕭 *Campo SS Giovanni e Paolo, Castello • Map E3 • Open 9:15am–6:30pm Mon–Sat, 1–6:30pm Sun • Admission charge*

Santa Maria dei Miracoli
A favourite among Venetians for weddings, Pietro Lombardo's showcase (1481–9) is resplendent again after restoration to deal with rising damp. The problem is not new – in Renaissance times marble slabs were affixed to the brick exterior with a cavity left for air flow. The ceiling gleams with gilt miniatures of holy figures *(see p95)*.

San Zaccaria
An intricately decorated 15th-century façade by Coducci and, inside, Giovanni Bellini's superb *Madonna and Saints* (1505) are highlights of this 9th-century church. The adjoining convent, now a police station, used to host puppet shows to entertain the nuns. 🕭 *Campo S Zaccaria, Castello • Map F4 • Open 10am–noon, 4–6pm Mon–Sat, 4–6pm Sun & public hols • Admission charge (chapels & crypt)*

San Giorgio Maggiore
Palladio's harmoniously proportioned church (1566–1610), inspired by Greek temple design, stands across the water from Piazza San Marco. The interior is offset by two dynamic paintings by Tintoretto from 1594, *The Last Supper* and *Gathering the Manna*, on the chancel walls. The bell tower offers views over Venice. Don't miss the monks' Gregorian chants every Sunday at 11am.
🕭 *Isola di S Giorgio Maggiore • Map F5 • Open daily (times can vary) • Admission charge (bell tower)*

San Giorgio Maggiore

Santa Maria della Salute
A remarkable Baroque church dominating the southernmost entrance to the Grand Canal, its silhouette has become one of Venice's most well-known landmarks.

For more on Venice artists and architects **See pp44–5**

Designed by Longhena in 1630, it has a spacious, light-filled interior, while the altar houses a precious Byzantine icon. Dramatic works by Titian and Tintoretto can be appreciated in the sacristy. ⌖ *Campo della Salute, Dorsoduro • Map D5 • Open 9am–noon, 3–5:30pm daily • Admission charge (sacristy)*

San Sebastiano
Paolo Veronese spent a large proportion of his life joyously decorating the ceiling, walls, organ doors and altar of this unassuming 16th-century church, and was buried among his colourful masterpieces, now beautifully restored *(see p89)*.

Madonna dell'Orto
Huge canvases by devout parishioner Tintoretto enhance this graceful Gothic church set on a quiet back canal. Two 1546 masterpieces flank the high altar, the gruesome *Last Judgment* and the soaring grandeur of *The Worship of the Golden Calf*. ⌖ *Campo Madonna dell'Orto, Cannaregio • Map D1 • Open 10am–5pm Mon–Sat, 1–5pm Sun • Admission charge*

San Pantalon

San Pantalon

Two treasures lurk behind a ramshackle façade: a nail from the True Cross in a Gothic altar and the overwhelming ceiling by Gian Antonio Fumiani, a labour of love (1680–1704) which ended when he purportedly plunged from the scaffolding to his death. ⌖ *Campo S Pantalon, Dorsoduro • Map K4 • Open 4–6pm Mon–Sat*

Top 10 Shrines and Tabernacles

1 Sottoportego de la Madonna
Pope Alexander III took refuge here in 1177, in flight from Emperor Barbarossa. ⌖ *Sant' Aponal, S Polo • Map D3*

2 Gondolier's Shrine
A 1583 Madonna greets boats approaching the bridge. ⌖ *Ponte della Paglia, S Marco • Map R5*

3 Corte Nova
Painted images over a lace-trimmed mantlepiece. ⌖ *Castello • Map G4*

4 Covered Passageway
The Virgin's protection has been implored here against plague and enemy attacks. ⌖ *Calle Zorzi, Castello • Map F4*

5 Scuola Grande della Misericordia
Carvings of laden boats invoke protection for the ferries, which set out from here. ⌖ *Cannaregio • Map D2*

6 Corte de Ca' Sarasina
Shrine dating back to the 1600s in memory of the dead. ⌖ *Castello • Map H5*

7 St Anthony
This 1668 "wardrobe" is full of fresh flower offerings. ⌖ *Calle Larga, Cannaregio • Map D2*

8 Ponte del Fontego
A Neo-Classical bridge featuring gondola *bas-reliefs*. ⌖ *Campo S Giustina, Castello • Map F3*

9 Gondola Traghetto Point
Madonna statue perched on a pole in the Grand Canal. ⌖ *S Tomà, S Polo • Map L4*

10 Boatmen's Pole
Tabernacle midway on the San Giuliano-Venice channel.

Left **Burano lacework** Centre **Museo Storico Navale** Right **Museo del Vetro**

🔟 Museums and Galleries

1 Accademia Galleries
See pp24–5.

2 Scuola Grande di San Rocco
The San Rocco confraternity has now been turned into a gallery to display its spectacular works by Tintoretto. The artist won the commission hands down – not content with a sketch, he completed an entire canvas. He then spent 23 years on the cycle of 60 inspired Old and New Testament scenes, culminating in the breathtaking *Crucifixion* (1565). They are the crowning glory of Tintoretto's life work *(see p81)*.

3 Fondazione Querini Stampalia
This unmissable Renaissance palace was the bequest of Giovanni Querini in 1868, the last member of the illustrious dynasty, on the condition that the library be made available "particularly in the evenings for the convenience of scholars". The immaculately restored palace-museum houses fascinating scenes of public and private life by Gabriel Bella and Pietro Longhi, as well as Carlo Scarpa's Modernist creations.
🔗 *Campo S Maria Formosa, Castello 5252 • Map E3 • Open 10am–6pm Tue–Sun (Fri & Sat until 10pm) • Admission charge*

4 Museo del Vetro
A phenomenal chandelier from 1864, constructed from 356 handmade pieces, weighing 330 kg (730 lb) and measuring nearly 7 m (23 ft) in circumference and 4 m (13 ft) high, is the star of this glass museum in the Palazzo Giustiniani. Other exhibits include Phoenician phials, blown vases, ruby chalices, exquisite mirrors and the famed kaleidoscopic beads once traded worldwide. 🔗 *Fondamenta Giustiniani 8, Murano • Map G2 • Open Apr–Oct: 10am–5pm Thu–Tue (Nov–Mar: 10am–4pm) • Admission charge*

5 Museo Correr
Priceless artworks and a miscellany of items on Venice's history are housed in this fine museum on Piazza San Marco *(see p18)*.

6 Scuola di San Giorgio degli Schiavoni
The finest work of Vittorio Carpaccio can be seen at the confraternity of the Slavs *(Schiavoni)*.

Fondazione Querini Stampalia

Slaying the dragon is one of the scenes from the lives of Dalmatian saints, executed in 1502.
◎ Calle dei Furlani, Castello 3259 • Map F4 • Open Apr–Oct: 9:30am–12:30pm, 3:30–6:30pm Tue–Sun (closed public hols & Sun pm in winter) • Admission charge

Museo Storico Navale
Watercraft galore are on display at the Historic Naval Museum, but the highlight is the replica of the Doge's ceremonial barge *Bucintoro*, richly decorated with allegorical statues.
◎ Campo S Biagio, Castello 2148 • Map G4 • Open 8:45am–1:30pm Mon–Sat • Admission charge

Ca' Pesaro Galleria d'Arte Moderna
A Baroque triumph of a palace whose interior, in contrast, accommodates works by leading European 19th- and 20th-century masters such as Marc Chagall and Gustave Klimt.
◎ Fondamenta Ca' Pesaro, S Croce 2076 • Map N1 • Open Tue–Sun (closed 1 Jan, 1 May & 25 Dec) • Admission charge

Museo del Merletto
A must for crafts enthusiasts is the lacemaking island of Burano and this precious display of more than 200 rare lace items, documenting a 500-year history.
◎ Piazza Baldassare Galuppi, Burano • Map H1 • Open Apr–Oct: 10am–5pm; Nov–Mar: 10am–4pm Wed–Mon • Admission charge

Studio with a Fruit Bowl (1942), Raoul Dufy, Ca' Pesaro

Museo di Icone
A rich if small collection of 14th–18th-century Byzantine icons is on display, some painted by Greek artists living in Venice.
◎ Ponte dei Greci, Castello 3412 • Map F4 • Open 9am–5pm daily (closed public hols) • Admission charge

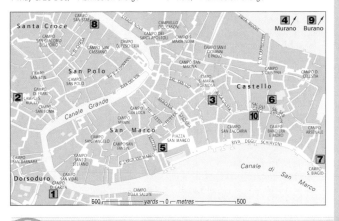

Left **Ca' d'Oro** Centre **Ca' Foscari** Right **Ca' Dario**

Venice Palaces

1 Doge's Palace
See pp12–15.

2 Ca' d'Oro
The original lapis-lazuli, vermilion and gold façade has long faded, but the breathtaking Gothic delicacy of this "golden palace" is intact, with exquisite marble tracery and arcaded loggias crafted by 15th-century stonemasons (see p95).

3 Ca' Foscari
Set on a strategic bend of the Grand Canal, this excellent example of late Gothic architecture has a series of mullioned windows facing the water, surmounted by an Istrian stone frieze. Once home to the long-ruling Doge Francesco Foscari, today it is part of the University of Venice. ⦾ Calle Foscari, Dorsoduro 3932 • Map L5 • Closed to public

4 Palazzo Vendramin-Calergi
This stately Renaissance residence by architects Lombardo and Coducci was home to a string of noble families including the Cretan merchant Calergi in 1589. Another famed tenant was German composer Richard Wagner, who spent his final years here. The palace is now home to the glittering City Casino (see p60).

5 Ca' Dario
Framed multicoloured round stones (tondi) embellish this privately owned asymmetrical palace dating from 1486. It was built for Giovanni Dario, ambassador to Constantinople, where he negotiated a peace treaty bringing long-term hostilities between Venice and the Turks to a temporary halt (see p21).

Palazzo Vendramin-Calergi

6 Ca' Rezzonico
This glittering palace adorned with Tiepolo ceiling frescoes, majestic Murano glass chandeliers and elaborate carved period furniture, has undergone extensive renovation. It is now home to the Museum of 18th-century Venetian Life. ⦾ Fondamenta Rezzonico, Dorsoduro 3136 • Map L5 • Open 10am–5pm Wed–Mon (6pm Apr–Oct) • Admission charge

7 Palazzo Mastelli
This eclectic delight, tucked away on a peaceful back canal of Cannaregio, was the abode of three merchant brothers from

Morea on the Peloponnese from 1112. Their turbaned likenesses in stone adorn neighbouring Campo dei Mori (see p95). A fascinating carved menagerie of lions, birds and a prominent camel can be picked out on the Gothic façade. ✎ *Rio della Madonna dell'Orto, Cannaregio 3932 • Map D1 • Closed to public*

Palazzi Contarini degli Scrigni

A 15th-century residence, enlarged by architect Vincenzo Scamozzi for the 17th-century proprietor Contarini "of the coffers" *(scrigni)*, so-called for the vast wealth of his family which resided in the Veneto region. The roof-top "folly" acted as a useful observatory for astronomers. ✎ *Calle Contarini Corfu, Dorsoduro 1057 • Map B5 • Closed to public*

Palazzi Barbaro

Cole Porter, Diaghilev, Monet and Whistler are just a few of the great names who figure among the past guests of this private double palace, courtesy of the 19th-century Curtis family from Boston. Henry James wrote *The Aspen Papers* here and used it as the setting for *The Wings of a Dove (see p51).* ✎ *Rio dell'Orso, S Marco 2840 • Map M6 • Closed to public*

Palazzo Pisani-Moretta

Venue of a fabulous masked ball during Carnival, when VIP guests still glide up in gondolas to the candlelit Gothic façade on the Grand Canal, as did the Tsar of Russia and Napoleon's Josephine in days gone by. Tiepolo and Guarana contributed to the interior Baroque decorations. ✎ *Ramo Pisani e Barbarigo, S Polo 2766 • Map M4 • Open for private functions only*

Top 10 Architectural Features of a Palazzo

1 Piano nobile
The high-ceilinged first floor of a palazzo hosts the sumptuous salons and family's living quarters.

2 Façade
Usually fronting a canal, this was the only exterior wall decorated with a costly stone overlay to impress visitors.

3 Funnel-shaped Chimneys
These and many other variations punctuate rooftops, their long shafts often running along outside walls.

4 Kitchen
This was always located on the ground floor for practical reasons.

5 Canal Entrance
Where the family's private gondolas were moored and visitors were received.

6 Central Well
This received filtered rain water for the palazzo's main water supply.

7 Entrance Portal
The importance of the main entrance was usually indicated by the distinctive family crest.

8 Enclosed Courtyard
This bustling area, usually with store rooms, was often used for the family's business transactions.

9 Altana Roof Terrace-Platform
These open-air areas were traditionally used for hanging out the washing or bleaching hair in the sun.

10 Land Access
With private gondolas, this was relatively unimportant, hence a narrow alley.

Left **Giovanni Bellini** Centre *Mary with Child* (1511–12), Giovanni Bellini Right **Titian self-portrait**

10 Artists in Venice

1 Giovanni Bellini
With his father Jacopo and brother Gentile, Giovanni (1430–1516) made Venice one of the greatest centres of Renaissance art. His trademarks are radiant Madonnas and serene St Peters.

2 Titian (Tiziano Vecellio)
A native of the Cadore region, whose Dolomite peaks often feature in his highly coloured works, Titian (1488–1576) studied under Giovanni Bellini.

3 Jacopo Tintoretto
The great Mannerist of the late Renaissance, Tintoretto (1518–94) produced huge, glowing canvases, seen at the Scuola Grande di San Rocco *(see p81)*.

4 Canaletto (Antonio Canal)
Famous for his landscapes of Venice and England, Canaletto (1697–1768) thrived under the patronage of the British consul Joseph Smith.

5 Paolo Veronese
Foremost painter of the Venetian School, Veronese's (1528–88) huge canvases, teeming with people, are on display in the Doge's Palace *(see pp12–15)*.

6 Giambattista Tiepolo
Tiepolo (1696–1770) is admired for his luminous poetic frescoes from the Rococo period, such as those in the Scuola Grande dei Carmini in Dorsoduro *(see p28)*.

7 Vittorio Carpaccio
This Renaissance master (1465–1525) delighted in detailed scenes of daily Venetian life. His narrative style and command of light characterize his cycles.

8 Giorgione
Despite his brief life, Giorgione (1477–1510) produced memorable mood works, surpassing his master, Giovanni Bellini.

9 Pietro Longhi
Longhi's (1702–85) witty scenes of the well-to-do in Venice can be admired at Ca' Rezzonico *(see p42)*.

10 Francesco Guardi
A prolific landscape painter, Guardi (1712–93) successfully captured the light and atmosphere of Venice in decline.

Rio dei Mendicanti (c.1723), Canaletto

For writers and Venice **See pp50–51**

Left **Libreria San Marco, Sansovino** Right **Il Redentore, Palladio**

🔟 Venice Architects

1 Jacopo Sansovino
Trained in Florence under sculptor Andrea Sansovino, whose name he adopted in homage, Jacopo (1486–1570) fled to Venice to escape the sacking of Rome. Of his outstanding architecture are the Libreria and Zecca *(see pp16–19)*.

2 Andrea Palladio
Regarded as one of the most influential architects of the western world, Palladio (1508–80) designed many Classical villas in the Veneto, along with the churches of Redentore and San Giorgio Maggiore in Venice.

3 Baldassare Longhena
The majestic Santa Maria della Salute, designed at the age of 26, is Longhena's (1598–1682) masterpiece, but his flamboyant style is recognizable in numerous churches and palaces, notably Ca' Rezzonico *(see p42)*.

4 Pietro Lombardo
A native of Lombardy, sculptor Pietro (1435–1515) took over as director of works at the Doge's Palace when Antonio Rizzo fled, accused of embezzlement. His trademark is a leafy *bas-relief* pattern, also seen on his Renaissance masterpiece, Santa Maria dei Miracoli *(see p95)*.

5 Mauro Coducci
The Renaissance designs of Lombard native Coducci (c.1440–1504) can be seen in the shape of Palazzo Vendramin-Calergi *(see p60)* and the churches of San Zaccaria and San Michele.

6 Bartolomeo Bon
Gothic sculptor and architect Bon's (1374–1464) designs were the basis for the church and Scuola di San Rocco. With his son Giovanni, he was also responsible for the Ca' d'Oro *(see p42)*.

7 Michele Sanmicheli
Original military fortification designs by this Mannerist architect (1484–1559) are to be found on the former Venetian islands of Crete and Cyprus, as well as monumental portals in his home town Verona *(see p124)*.

8 Antonio Da Ponte
Renowned for the landmark Rialto bridge *(see p28)*, this engineer and architect (1512–95) also made numerous contributions to the Doge's Palace *(see p12–15)*.

9 Giannantonio Selva
In Venice, French-inspired Selva (1757–1819) is best remembered for the elegant Fenice theatre, though he also played a hand in works of the Napoleonic era including restructuring the Accademia Galleries.

10 Carlo Scarpa
Modernist Scarpa (1906–78) admirably reorganized both the Accademia collection and the Querini Stampalia along Japanese-inspired lines.

For Venice churches See pp38–9

Left **Ponte degli Scalzi** Centre **Rialto Bridge** Right **Ponte dei Pugni**

🔟 Bridges

1 Bridge of Sighs
This evocatively named bridge once led convicts from the Doge's Palace to the adjacent prisons *(see p13)*. 🗺 Map R5

2 Rialto Bridge
The design of this most famous Venetian bridge at the narrowest point of the Grand Canal was hotly contested – leading 16th-century architects Michelangelo, Sansovino and Palladio all entered the competition, but lost out to the imposing winning project of 1588–91 by Antonio da Ponte. There were two previous bridges on this site; a timber bridge which collapsed in 1444 under the weight of a crowd, then a drawbridge, raised for the passage of tall-masted sailing ships *(see p28)*. 🗺 Map P3

3 Ponte degli Scalzi
One of the city's most marvellous lookout points, over fascinating palaces and boats, can be had from this elegant 40-m (130-ft) long bridge,

7 m (23 ft) above the Grand Canal. Named after the nearby monastery of bare-footed monks, this 1934 structure in Istrian stone by Eugenio Miozzi replaced an Austrian-built iron bridge. 🗺 Map J1

4 Ponte della Libertà
Truth and irony combine in the name of this 3.6-km (2-mile) "Bridge of Freedom": the first full link between the mainland and Venice was put in place in 1933, when Italy was living under Fascism. The construction was preceded 86 years earlier by the Austrian-built railway bridge across the lagoon. Before that, the city relied entirely on boats. 🗺 Map A1

5 Ponte dei Tre Archi
A favourite subject for artists, this unusual three-arched high bridge dating from 1688 crosses the Cannaregio canal close to where it joins the lagoon. It was the work of engineer Andrea Tirali, nicknamed Tiranno (the tyrant) by his employees. 🗺 Map B1

Tre Ponti, Santa Croce

For getting around Venice by boat See p135

Ponte dei Pugni

Fistfights *(pugni)* between rival clans took place here until 1705 when they were outlawed for their violence *(see p90)*. Stone footprints marked the starting point of the combat, but contestants usually ended up in the canal. ◈ *Map K5*

Ponte delle Tette

When an increase in the practice of sodomy was recorded in the 1400s, the city's prostitutes were encouraged to display their feminine wares at the windows over the "Bridge of Breasts". ◈ *Map M2*

Bridge with No Parapet

One of only two remaining bridges with no side protection, this one spans a quiet side canal in Cannaregio. The other is the Ponte del Diavolo on Torcello. ◈ *Map D2*

Tre Ponti

Not three but five interlocking bridges span the Rio Nuovo canal near Piazzale Roma. The timber and stone structures afford views taking in 13 other bridges. ◈ *Map B3*

Ponte Lungo

Marvellous views of Piazza San Marco should entice visitors to this 33-m (110-ft) long iron bridge. Halfway along Giudecca, from 1340 it served as a link with newly reclaimed tidal flats. ◈ *Map C6*

Bridge with No Parapet

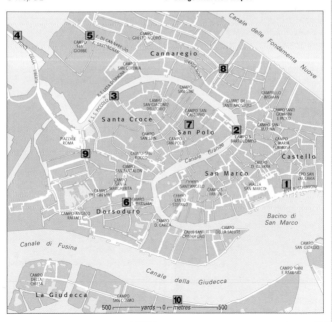

Left **Parco Savorgnan** Centre **Cloister of Sant'Apollonia** Right **Campo della Maddalena**

🔟 Hidden Venice

1 Parco Savorgnan
A well-hidden haven of chirping birds in towering shady trees, signposted from Campo San Geremia and Fondamenta Savorgnan. Part of the park once belonged to Palazzo Savorgnan, now a school, which backs on to it, and boasted statues, citrus trees and Roman stonework.
🔾 *Cannaregio • Map B2*

2 Rio Terrà Rampani
This quiet thoroughfare, around the corner from Ponte delle Tette, is usually referred to as the "Carampane" (Ca' Rampani), alias the red-light district as of 1421. Venice had some 11,600 officially registered courtesans in the 1500s. A particularly narrow alley, Calle della Raffineria, site of a 1713 sugar refinery, runs off it.
🔾 *S Polo • Map M2*

Rio Terrà Rampani

3 Corte del Duca Sforza
A picturesque courtyard opening onto the Grand Canal, it was named after the duke of Milan who took over a partially constructed palace here in 1461. However, work did not go much further than the diamond-point ashlar on the façade. The artist Titian used it as a studio when working on the Doge's Palace.
🔾 *S Marco • Map L6*

4 Celestia to Bacini
A lengthy atmospheric walkway in a somewhat neglected zone of Castello, fronting the lagoon. The path clings to the wall of the ancient Arsenale shipyards *(see p101)*, and leads to a cluster of workers' dwellings.
🔾 *Castello • Map G3*

5 Corte dell'Anatomia
This quiet courtyard took its name from the anatomy theatre which existed here as of 1368. In 1671, a College of Anatomy was also established over the bridge in Campo San Giacomo dell'Orio, now an isolated building with a pretty vine-covered trellis.
🔾 *S Croce • Map L2*

6 Campiello del Remer
This delightful square faces the Grand Canal and took its name from the local oarmakers. It boasts several Byzantine features, notably the wellhead of Verona stone and pointed ogee arches from a 13th-century palace.
🔾 *Cannaregio • Map P2*

7 Cloister of Sant'Apollonia
Venice's only authentic Romanesque cloister has a courtyard with twin-columned arcades, now part of a church museum.
◈ Castello • Map R4

8 Campo della Celestia
Now a tranquil residential square, in the 13th century it saw plenty of action when the sisters of a Cistercian convent gained a riotous reputation. Under Napoleon an archive of city affairs took over the building.
◈ Castello • Map G3

Calle del Paradiso

9 Calle del Paradiso
Though slightly lop-sided, a delicately sculptured 15th-century arch representing the Virgin and her devotees never fails to delight. The attractive alley is lined with medieval-style timber overhangs.
◈ Castello • Map R3

10 Campo della Maddalena
Unchanged since medieval times, this lovely raised square often doubles as a film set. Its modest houses are topped with chimneys in varying styles.
◈ Cannaregio • Map D2

Top 10 Animals in Venice

1 Pigeons
Piazza San Marco wouldn't be the same without them, but their droppings play havoc with the stonework.

2 Lions
Symbol of Venice and St Mark, abundant statuary and paintings of lions in varying forms fill the city.

3 Cats
The city's feline population is pampered and fed by affectionate Venetians.

4 Rats
Rare, thanks to imported Syrian cats in the past, replaced by an effective council eradication campaign.

5 Horses
Once ridden around town by the Venetian nobility, even up the Campanile via a ramp.

6 Dogs
By law dogs in Venice must be muzzled, kept on a leash and cleaned up after at all times.

7 Seagulls
Self-appointed garbage collectors, they do an admirable job around the markets.

8 Cormorants
Hundreds of elegant jet-black waterfowl inhabit the lagoon, to the chagrin of the fishermen.

9 Rhinoceroses
One of the many exotic circus animals portrayed on canvas by 18th-century artist Pietro Longhi.

10 Elephants
Incredibly, a runaway elephant from an 1819 circus took refuge in a church, and cannon fire was needed to dispatch it.

Left **Shakespeare** Centre left **Carlo Goldoni** Centre right **Thomas Mann** Right **Ernest Hemingway**

Writers and Venice

1 Carlo Goldoni
"Italy's Molière" (1707–93) is celebrated at the Venetian theatre named in his honour *(see p66)*. Performances of his lively, witty comedies are staged in Venetian dialect and peopled with recognizable local characters. The prolific playwright moved to Paris and was rewarded with a royal pension, but he died destitute due to the French Revolution.

2 Thomas Mann
The sombre 1912 novel *Death in Venice* was both written and set in Venice and the Lido resort by the German Nobel Prize-winner (1875–1955). It tells the story of an ageing writer in dire need of relaxation who visits the city, but in the wake of an impossible infatuation slowly succumbs to the spreading cholera epidemic and dies.

Johann Wolfgang von Goethe

3 William Shakespeare
Although he never visited Italy, let alone Venice, the English Bard (1564–1616) used accounts by contemporary travellers for the plots of *The Merchant of Venice* and *Othello*, portraying a city buzzing with trade and intrigue. *Romeo and Juliet* is set in Verona *(see p124)*.

4 Thomas Coryate
The very first English-language traveller to write a detailed description of Venice, this eccentric gentleman from Somerset, England (1577–1617) compiled *Crudities, with Observations of Venice* (1611): "Such is the rarenesse of the situation of Venice, that it doth even amaze and drive into admiration all strangers that upon their first arrival behold the same."

5 Johann Wolfgang von Goethe
The story goes that this German literary giant (1749–1832) had his first ever view of the sea from Venice's Campanile. Attracted by the lands south of the Alps, his first visit was an experience of personal renewal, the account published as *Italian Journey* (1786–8).

6 Lord Byron
Eccentricities such as a menagerie of foxes and monkeys, not to mention swimming feats in the Grand Canal, made

For more on Shakespeare's Verona See p124

the English Romantic poet (1788–1824) something of a legend during his three-year sojourn here. His Venice-inspired work included *The Two Foscari* and the fourth canto of his autobiographical work *Childe Harold's Pilgrimage*.

John Ruskin

The meticulous if opinionated labour of love of this British art critic (1819–1900), *The Stones of Venice*, was the first work to focus the attention of visitors on the city's unique architectural heritage and Gothic style, as opposed to the art. The book was largely the outcome of an 1849 visit.

John Ruskin

Henry James

The leitmotif of this US novelist (1843–1916) was the contrast between what he saw as the spontaneity of the New World and the staidness of Europe. Between 1872 and 1909 he compiled *Italian Hours*, a "travel diary" with plenty of comments on Venice.

Ernest Hemingway

This US Nobel Prize winner (1899–1961) experienced Italy first-hand as a volunteer ambulance driver during World War I (recounted in *A Farewell to Arms*) and he was wounded near Treviso. *Across the River and into the Trees* is set in Harry's Bar (see p21).

Charles Dickens

The great English novelist (1812–70) spent a brief period in Venice during a tour of Italy, and the city inspired a dream sequence in his work *Pictures from Italy* (1846).

Top 10 Background Reads

1 Venice, Jan Morris
An expert account of the delights of the city and its maritime history.

2 Venice, an Anthology Guide, Milton Grundy
A guide around town, seen through the eyes of famous writers.

3 Ruskin's Venice, editor Arnold Whittick
A very readable version of Ruskin's landmark work.

4 Death in Venice, Thomas Mann
A portrayal of desire and decadence amid the fog.

5 Stone Virgin, Barry Unsworth
A mystery involving the 15th-century statue of a famous courtesan.

6 Casanova, or the Art of Happiness, Lydia Flem
An inspired biography of the famous seducer (see p52).

7 Dead Lagoon, Michael Dibdin
Detective Aurelio Zen navigates Venice's murky waters wrought with unease and intrigue.

8 The Architecture of Venice, Deborah Howard
An unbeatable architectural classic.

9 Venice: A Maritime Republic, Frederic C. Lane
A comprehensive history of the city's maritime prowess.

10 Acqua Alta, Donna Leon
From the best-selling mystery series featuring detective Guido Brunetti.

Left **Marco Polo** Centre **Daniele Manin** Right **Giovanni Casanova**

🔟 Outstanding Venetians

1 Marco Polo
Legendary Cathay and the kingdom of the mighty Kublai Khan took pride of place in explorer Marco Polo's best-selling account of his 20-year odyssey to the Far East, *Il milione*. Son of a Venetian merchant, Marco Polo (1254–1324) is responsible for the introduction of pasta and window blinds to the western world.

2 Antonio Vivaldi
Vivaldi (1678–1741) was both an accomplished musician and an influential composer. Of his 500 concertos, *The Four Seasons* is the best known, though 10 were transcribed by J.S. Bach. Vivaldi spent extended periods teaching music at the Pietà home for girls *(see p66)*.

Prolific Venetian composer Antonio Vivaldi

3 Giovanni Casanova
This marvellous romantic figure (1725–98) was variously a diplomat, scholar, trainee priest, adventurer, gambler, notary's clerk, violinist, womanizer, exile, millionaire, writer and spy. Casanova was imprisoned in the Doge's Palace *(see pp12–15)* on charges of being a magician, from where he effected an infamously daring escape.

4 Claudio Monteverdi
This late Renaissance madrigalist (1567–1643) is attributed with the introduction of the solo voice to theatre. His opera *Proserpina Rapita* was the first to be performed in Venice. After long periods at the court of the Gonzagas, he accepted an appointment at the Basilica San Marco and worked for the Scuola Grande di San Rocco *(see p81)*.

5 John Cabot
Italian navigator Giovanni Caboto, or John Cabot (1450–99), and his sons were authorized by Henry VII of England to search for new lands with the aim of furthering trade. Believing himself on the northeast coast of Asia, he discovered Newfoundland in Canada and claimed it for England, opening up cod fishing.

6 Elena Lucrezia Corner Piscopia
It was inconceivable for the church in 1678 that a woman should teach religion, so the University of Padua awarded this child prodigy and the first woman graduate (1646–84) a degree in philosophy, instead of one in theology to which she aspired.

7 Daniele Manin

Organizer of the 1848 rebellion against Austrian rule, the Venetian patriot (1804–57) is commemorated by a statue in Campo Manin. An independent "republic" was declared and survived 17 months of bombardments and even cholera, concluding with Manin's exile to Paris.

8 Paolo Sarpi

When the pope excommunicated Venice for insubordination, involving restrictions on church construction and the refusal to hand over two priests on criminal charges, Sarpi (1552–1623) resolved the rupture. A patriot and theologian, he was an advocate of division between State and Church.

9 Caterina Cornaro

This Venetian noblewoman (1454–1510) married the king of Cyprus then allegedly poisoned him, thus securing the strategic island for Venice. Her return to the city was an occasion of great pomp, recalled to this day in a waterborne procession during the Regata

Queen of Cyprus, Caterina Cornaro

Storica (see p62). Cornaro's reward was the hilltown of Asolo.

10 Luigi Nono

This musician (1924–90) made milestone progress in the field of electronic music, and an archive named after him was set up in Venice in 1993. A committed Communist, his works were often provocative.

Top 10 Foreign Communities

1 Greeks
Since 1498 the longest surviving group, still active with their own church.

2 Armenians
Fleeing Turkish invasion, in 1717 the close-knit religious group was granted an island by the Republic (see p116).

3 Dalmatians (Slavs)
Active traders whose boats gave their name to the Riva degli Schiavoni (see p101).

4 Turks
Sworn political enemies of Venice, the Republic still rented them a trade centre between 1621 and 1898.

5 Jews
The Spanish Inquisition triggered the move here for many Jews expelled from other European countries.

6 Albanians
Calle degli Albanesi near Piazza San Marco is named in honour of this large 15th-century community.

7 Germans
The former German trade headquarters Fondaco dei Tedeschi attracted artists such as Albrecht Dürer.

8 British
Extended sojourns here were mandatory for British upper classes during the 19th-century Grand Tour.

9 French
Impressionist Monet and writers Théophile Gautier and Marcel Proust were attracted to the city in the late 1800s.

10 Americans
Leading literary figures and patrons of the arts have paid long-term visits since the 19th century.

Left **Macello façade** Right **Cantieri Navali research centre**

Historic Conversions

1 Zecca

This elegant waterfront mint was designed by Jacopo Sansovino *(see p45)* and completed in 1545, although a former mint had existed here since 1277. Operations came to a halt in 1870 and in 1905 the building became the home of the Marciana Library. ⊗ *Piazza S Marco, S Marco 3 • Map Q5 • Closed to the public*

2 Cotonificio

Now occupied by the university architecture faculty, these former cotton mills are a fine example of re-using the city's derelict industrial buildings. The mills and their 1,000 employees were active from 1883 to 1960. ⊗ *Fondamenta Bari, Dorsoduro 2196 • Map A4 • Closed to the public*

3 Arsenale

The 300-m (980-ft) long Corderie building in the historic Arsenale shipyards is the perfect setting for the Biennale Arts show held here since 1980 *(see p101)*, but in the past endless lengths of hemp rope were manufactured here. The Gaggiandre docks and 16th-century sailmaking area were adapted into a theatre in 1999 *(see p101)*.

4 Molino Stucky

Plans are afoot to convert this impressive Hanseatic Gothic flour mill dominating the Giudecca Canal into a conference and hotel complex. Built between 1897–1920, workers pale-faced from flour were a common sight until 1954 when operations ceased. ⊗ *Campo S Biagio, Giudecca 810 • Map C6*

5 Magazzini del Sale

The lagoon's salt pans largely contributed to the Republic's trade monopoly and salt was stored in these cavernous 14th-century warehouses. The buildings now store boats. ⊗ *Zattere, Dorsoduro 258–266 • Map D5 • Closed to the public*

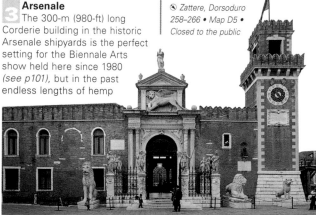

Arsenale façade, Castello

Deposito del Megio

Few children can boast such a historic home for their primary schooling. A stone lion presides over this former state grain store, essential during the 1559 famine. It was converted in 1921–22. ◈ *Calle del Megio, S Croce 1779 • Map M1 • Closed to the public*

Macello

The Neo-Classical former abattoir, its façade aptly decorated with bucranium (sculpted ox skulls), was restructured by the university when it was granted the premises in 1986. ◈ *Fondamenta di S Giobbe, Cannaregio 879 • Map B1 • Closed to the public*

Cotonificio, now a university faculty

Cantieri Navali

A state-of-the-art research centre on coastal and marine technology now accounts for another vast area of the Arsenale. The 16th–19th-century shipyards, set amid a lush garden, were converted in 1991. ◈ *Arsenale, Castello 2737/F • Map H3 • Closed to the public*

CIGA Warehouses

One of the city's best public sports facilities is located in this series of modest repositories, including an indoor swimming pool, gym and bowls facilities. ◈ *S Alvise, Cannaregio 3190 • Map C1 • Open daily (hours vary) • Admission charge*

Junghans Factory

New York-style loft apartments have been created from an old clock factory – one of many conversion projects taking place on Giudecca. ◈ *Giudecca 373 • Map D6 • Closed to the public*

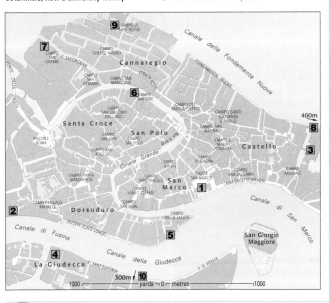

Left **Cantina Do Mori** Centre **Osteria alla Botte** Right **Al Bottegon**

🔟 Osterie (Wine Bars)

1 Cantina Do Mori

Rows of copper polenta pots hang overhead in this dark, popular bar, billed as the city's oldest *osteria*. The affable owners pour wine directly from huge demijohns and serve delicate postage stamp-sized ham and salad sandwiches *(francobolli)*. ◈ *Calle dei Do Mori, S Polo 429 • Map N2*

2 Osteria alla Patatina (Al Ponte)

Piping hot wedges of fried potato served on skewers *(patatine)* are the mainstay here, though don't neglect the other tasty morsels, such as delicately battered vegetable strips, to be washed down with some Veneto red or white wines served from bottles or demi-johns. ◈ *Ponte S Polo, S Polo 2741 • Map M3*

Osteria alla Patatina (Al Ponte)

3 Banco Giro, Osteria da Andrea

A welcome watering hole in a converted market store at Rialto, where Andrea guarantees quality Italian vintages and tasty nibbles. On the seasonal menu is *carpaccio di branzino alla rucola* (marinated sea bass with rocket). ◈ *Campo S Giacometto, S Polo 122 • Map P2*

4 Osteria del Sacro e Profano

Well worth hunting out near Rialto, this rustic-looking *osteria* is the haunt of international artists who happily mingle with the locals. Wines from the Veneto and Friuli are served with traditional snacks such as *uova con acciughe* (hard-boiled egg with anchovy). ◈ *Ramo secondo del Parangon, S Polo 502 • Map P2*

5 Osteria Sora al Ponte

A boisterous establishment run by a market family ensures an entertaining visit. Traditional fare such as *bisatei fritti* (fried baby eels) and tripe are worth trying with your carafe of wine. ◈ *Ponte delle Becarie, S Polo 1588 • Map N2*

6 Osteria alla Frasca

Billed as the site where Titian kept his paints and canvases, this tiny picturesque bar serves drinks and snacks on a vine-covered terrace in summer. ◈ *Corte della Carità, Cannaregio 5176 • Map E2*

7 Enoteca do Colonne

Animated neighbourhood bar with all manner of counter food ranging from *baccalà* (salted cod) on crusty bread or hearty *musetto* sausage, served with great smiles by the affable young owners. Decent selection of Veneto wines too. ⓝ *Rio Terrà del Cristo, Cannaregio 1814C • Map C2*

8 Osteria alla Botte

You have to fight your way through the locals here, attracted by the lively atmosphere and counter over-flowing with drinkable local wines and appetizing snacks such as fried sardines in breadcrumbs. ⓝ *Calle della Bissa, S Marco 5482 • Map Q3*

Wine cask

9 Trattoria Ca' d'Oro alla Vedova

Young enterprising management has recently taken over this timber-panelled establishment which has been serving mouth-watering counter snacks *(cicheti)* such as crispy battered artichokes and quaffable wine for longer than any of the regulars can remember. ⓝ *Calle del Pistor, Cannaregio 3912 • Map D2*

10 Al Bottegon

Not far from the Accademia Bridge, join the locals at this family-run specialist wine cellar that serves excellent Prosecco at the stand-up bar. Simple nibbles to accompany the wine include *mortadella* sausage and *panini* rolls filled with *sopressa*, a local salami. ⓝ *Fondamenta Nani, Dorsoduro 992 • Map C5*

Top 10 Drinks

1 Spritz
Unrivalled Venetian favourite of white wine with a splash of Bitter, Aperol or Select (apéritif brands) and a shot of mineral water.

2 Prosecco
Excellent naturally sparkling dry white wine from the hills around Conegliano and Valdobbiadene.

3 Bellini
Smooth fresh peach juice and sparkling Prosecco blend, invented by Cipriani of Harry's Bar *(see p21)*.

4 Red Wine
An *ombra* means a small glass of house wine, other-wise try quality Cabernet, Valpolicella or Amarone.

5 White Wine
Soave and Pinot Grigio are worthwhile alternatives to house varieties.

6 Mineral Water
Widely consumed in Italy, either sparkling *(con gas)* or still *(senza gas)*. Tap water is *acqua dal rubinetto*.

7 Fruit Drinks
These can be ordered as *spremuta* (freshly squeezed juice) or *succo di frutta* (bottled nectars).

8 Coffee
Straight *espresso*, frothy *cappuccino* or *caffè latte* in a tall glass with hot milk.

9 Tea
Usually served with a slice of lemon, though herbal tea *(infuso)*, such as camo-mile, is common.

10 After-dinner Sgroppino
A well-kept local secret concocted with lemon sorbet, vodka and Prosecco.

For Venice nightspots See pp60–61

Left **Fiaschetteria Toscana** Right **Do Forni**

🔟 Places to Eat in Venice

1 Hotel Cipriani
Restaurant guests are ferried over to this hotel-restaurant by the Cipriani's private launch from Piazza San Marco for a memorable gastronomic experience at two venues. The fixed-price buffet lunch will set you back a hefty sum, but the setting is wonderful. One speciality is *tagliolini gratinati al prosciutto* (ribbon pasta with ham, browned in the oven). Ⓢ *Giudecca 10 • Map E6 • 041 520 77 44 • Closed Nov–Mar • €€€€€*

2 Da Fiore
Reservations are essential at this sophisticated restaurant, where the owners base the day's menu on what is fresh at the market. They might have *pappardelle con ostriche e zafferano* (flat ribbon pasta with oysters and saffron), or *moleche fritte con polenta* (fried soft-shelled crab with cornmeal). Ⓢ *Calle del Scaleter, S Polo 2202/A • Map M3 • 041 721 308 • Closed Sun–Mon, 3 weeks in Dec, 3 weeks in Aug • No disabled access • €€€€€*

3 Grand Canal, Hotel Monaco
Traditional Venetian and Italian cuisine of a very high standard, including freshly made pasta with shrimp and seafood risotto, accompanied by the best of European wines. The setting, a terrace on the Grand Canal, is stunning. Ⓢ *Calle Vallaresso, S Marco 1325 • Map Q6 • 041 520 02 11 • €€€€€*

4 Fiaschetteria Toscana
Historic locale with a courtyard and superb food. *Filetto di rombo con carciofi* (turbot fillet with artichokes) and *tagliolini neri al ragù di astice* (black cuttlefish pasta with lobster) stand out. Ⓢ *Salizzada S Giovanni Grisostomo, Cannaregio 5719 • Map E3 • 041 528 52 81 • Closed Tue & Wed L, late Jul–late Aug • €€€€*

5 Corte Sconta
This former *osteria* is now a trendy restaurant that serves memorable seafood in a pretty "hidden courtyard" *(corte sconta)*. Don't miss *pincia*, the local bread pudding, for dessert. The house wine is also wonderful. Booking ahead is essential. Ⓢ *Calle del Pestrin, Castello 3886 • Map F4 • 041 522 70 24 • Closed Sun–Mon, Jan, mid-Jul–mid-Aug • €€€€–€€€€€*

Grand Canal, Hotel Monaco

Do Forni

Right by Piazza San Marco, frequented by business people and politicians. Customers enter an imitation Orient Express dining car to be greeted by displays of glistening seafood. Book ahead. ® *Calle Specchieri, S Marco 468 • Map Q4 • 041 523 21 48 • No disabled access • €€€€€*

Vini da Gigio

Tiny restaurant with a great reputation. The owner prides himself on his Italian and foreign wines to accompany dishes such as *tagliata di tonno* (fresh tuna fillet with herbs). Booking is recommended. ® *Fondamenta S Felice, Cannaregio 3628/a • Map D2 • 041 528 51 40 • Closed Mon & Tue, 2 weeks in Jan & in Aug • No disabled access • €€€*

L'Incontro

Friendly restaurant specializing in Sardinian meat dishes such as *maialino alla sarda* (suckling pig with maquis herb myrtle). ® *Rio Terrà Canal, Dorsoduro 3062/A • Map K5 • 041 522 24 04 • Closed Mon, Tue L, 2 weeks Jan • €€€*

La Colombina

Tucked away just off the Strada Nuova, this modern eatery offers a choice of 140 Italian wines, innovative Tuscan and Veneto cuisine and a pleasant courtyard. ® *Corte del Pegolotto, Cannaregio 1828 • Map C2 • 041 275 06 22 • Closed at lunchtime • €€€*

Trattoria alla Madonna

Traditional restaurant with an inspiring display of fresh seafood: *spaghetti con nero* (with cuttlefish ink sauce) and *anguilla fritta* (fried eel). No bookings, so expect to queue. ® *Calle della Madonna, S Polo 594 • Map P3 • 041 522 38 24 • Closed Wed, 25 Dec–31 Jan, 5–20 Aug • No disabled access • €€*

Top 10 What to Eat

Carpaccio

Raw beef sliced thin and sprinkled with flakes of Parmesan cheese or rocket (arugula).

Sarde in Saor

Fried sardines marinated in a sweet and sour mixture of onions, currants and pine nuts, invented for sailors at sea for lengthy periods.

Antipasto di Frutti di Mare

Seafood platter of baby octopus, anchovies, shrimp or whatever else is in season.

Prosciutto e Melone

The sweetness of wedges of fresh rock melon is contrasted by the slightly salty cured Parma ham.

Risotto di Pesce

Clams, mussels, shrimp and assorted fish in a heavenly creamy rice dish.

Pasta con il Nero di Seppia

Usually spaghetti, combined with a rich sauce of tomato and cuttlefish, thoroughly blackened with the ink.

Fegato alla Veneziana

Calves' liver Venetian-style cooked slowly with onions and vinegar.

Grilled Fish

Such as *coda di rospo* (monkfish) or *pesce spada* (swordfish) from the south.

Grilled Vegetables

Radicchio (red chicory) in winter, *zucchini* (courgettes) and *melanzane* (aubergine/eggplant) in summer, and roasted *peperoni* (peppers).

Tiramisù

Dessert with a creamy sauce of eggs and mascarpone between layers of sponge drenched in coffee or liqueur.

 For a guide to restaurant prices **See pages 79, 85, 93, 99, 105, 113, 119 and 129**

Left **Le Bistrot de Venise** Right **Bacaro Jazz**

🔟 Nightspots

1 Paradiso Perduto
Call it animated or just plain noisy, but live ethnic music, flowing wine and simple seafood are all part of the vibrant atmosphere of "Lost Paradise". Always full to the (low) rafters, the exuberant crowd often spills out onto the canalside where tables are set up in spring and summer – weather permitting of course. ⊗ *Fondamenta della Misericordia, Cannaregio 2540 • Map D2*

2 Centrale
A thoughtful use of candles and soft music helps to create a pleasant and welcoming ambience to this lounge bar and restaurant. They serve imaginative and sometimes somewhat innovative Mediterranean cuisine each evening until 2am. ⊗ *Piscina Frezzaria, San Marco 1659 • 041 296 0664 • Map P5*

3 Fiddler's Elbow Irish Pub
Marvellous, lively atmos-phere and great Guinness,

Fiddler's Elbow Irish Pub

naturally. You can always count on action here – a concert of Irish music in the cosy square, a maxi screen for football games, while at Carnival and, of course, St Patrick's Day, this is *the* place to be. ⊗ *Campiello dei Testori, Cannaregio 3847 • Map D2*

4 Chet Bar
One of the many lively music bars that can be found in Campo S Margherita. Chet Bar is a popular joint and is, as the name clearly indicates, dedicated to that great trumpet player Chet Baker. ⊗ *Campo S Margherita, Dorsuduro 3684 • 041 296 0664 • Map K5 • Closed Nov–Mar*

5 Casinò Municipale, Palazzo Vendramin-Calergi
A magnificent start to an exciting evening – a special ACTV launch from Piazzale Roma transports hopeful clients down the Grand Canal to the landing stage of the beautiful Renaissance palace, alias City Casino, for a glittering night at the tables or the slot machines. It is also a short walk from the San Marcuola ferry stop. ⊗ *Campiello Vendramin, Cannaregio 2040 • Map C2*

6 Martini Scala-Club Piano Bar
This chic locale is the only place in Venice where you can enjoy high-quality cuisine and wine until the small hours of the morning, while being entertained by live music in air-conditioned

comfort. No sleeveless tops or shorts, for men or women, are allowed. ◈ *Campo S Fantin, S Marco 1980 • Map N5 • Closed Tue*

Casinò Municipale

Bacaro Jazz

An enthusiastic multilingual welcome is extended to all visitors in this lively wine bar that never seems to close. It boasts almost non-stop service, an extended "happy hour" from 4–7pm and a delicious assortment of Spanish-style *tapas* snack meals to accompany the wine. ◈ *Salizzada Fontego dei Tedeschi, S Marco 5546 • Map Q3*

Le Bistrot de Venise

An eclectic programme of events here never ceases to entertain, from poetry readings to art exhibitions and wine and food events. An added bonus is superb wine and a fascinating menu of dishes based on traditional 15th-century recipes. ◈ *Calle dei Fabbri, S Marco 4685 • Map P4 • 041 523 66 51 • Closed 22–25 Dec • www.bistrotdevenise.com*

Cantina Vecia Carbonera

However late in the evening, you can turn up here and count on live music, a good glass of wine and a crusty *crostino* topped with anchovies or cheese. On summer evenings locals row up to the waterside entrance. ◈ *Ponte Sant'Antonio, Cannaregio 2329 • Map D2*

Piccolo Mondo

This tiny club, which does not open until 11pm, has a wonderful laidback atmosphere. Entrance close to the Accademia gallery. ◈ *Calle Contarini Corfù, Dorsoduro 1056/A • Map L6*

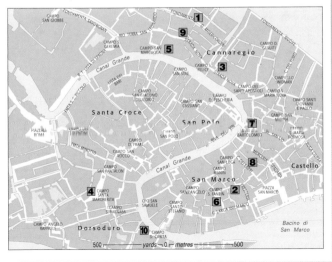

Left **Carnival costumes** Centre **Vogalonga** Right **Regata Storica**

Festivals and Events

1 Carnival
An unmissable 10-day extravaganza that takes over the city as a countdown to Lent. The streets mill with costumed and masked local "nobility" or crazily attired visitors. It gets off to a flying start with the *Volo della Colombina* (flight of the dove), when either an acrobat or a cardboard dove is launched from the Campanile in Piazza San Marco, showering on-lookers with confetti. The grand finale is the explosive Mardi Gras.
◈ *Feb–Mar, concluding on Shrove Tue, 40 days before Easter*

2 Regata Storica
The word regatta originated in Venice so what better place to enjoy the year's most spectacular event? Ornately decorated boats propelled by costumed oarsmen parade down the Grand Canal bearing passengers dressed as historical dignitaries. A series of furiously contested regattas follows. ◈ *1st Sun in Sep*

3 Vogalonga
A colourful armada of rowing craft from all over the world embarks on a 32-km (20-mile) non-competitive route around the lagoon's scattered islands. The "Long Row" is a great experience for both participants and on-lookers, who line the Canale di Cannaregio towards midday to cheer on the breathtaking final stretch down the Grand Canal.
◈ *May: Sun after Ascension*

4 Festa del Redentore
People crowd on to all available watercraft, decorated with paper lanterns and greenery, for a feast of roast duck and watermelon, followed by a midnight fireworks display. It all takes place near Palladio's church on Giudecca *(see p45)* to commemorate the end of the 1576 plague. For those on foot, a temporary pontoon bridge stretches from the Zattere over the Giudecca canal. ◈ *Mid-Jul: Sat*

5 Biennale Art Exhibition
The world's leading international art bonanza is held on a two-yearly basis. The leafy gardens in eastern Castello are the principal venue, supplemented by the Corderie building in the Arsenale *(see p54)*. ◈ *Jun–Nov*

Venice Marathon

Madonna della Salute

Venetians make a pilgrimage to Longhena's church on the Grand Canal *(see p38)* every winter, to give thanks for the end of the 1630 plague. The area assumes a festive atmosphere with stalls selling candy floss and balloons. ✪ *21 Nov*

Venice Marathon

One of the world's most beautiful marathon routes. Runners from all parts of the globe begin this classic 42-km (26-mile) race at Villa Pisani on the Brenta waterway, cross the causeway to Venice, the Zattere and San Marco, and finish near the public gardens in Castello. ✪ *Late Oct*

Su e Zo per i Ponti

Anyone can take part in this leisurely non-competitive walk or run "up and down the bridges". A variety of official routes can be followed, and all participants receive a medal on finishing. ✪ *Late Mar/Apr: 4th Sun in Lent*

La Sensa

Head for the Riviera di San Nicolò at the Lido *(see p115)* to watch this ancient ceremony of "Venice wedding the Sea". A costumed "doge" casts a ring into the sea amid a procession of celebratory boats. Symbolizing Venice's maritime supremacy, the Sensa has been staged since Venice took Istria and Dalmatia in AD 997. ✪ *May: Ascension Day*

Festa di San Rocco

The feast day of St Roch, the French saint adopted by the confraternity for alleviating the 1576–7 plague, is celebrated each year at the Scuola Grande di San Rocco *(see p81)*. A mass and evening concert conclude the festivities. ✪ *16 Aug*

Top 10 Sports in Venice

1 Rowing

Immensely popular Venetian pastime practised standing-up. Join the oldest club Canottieri Bucintoro. ✪ *Zattere, Dorsoduro • Map D5*

2 Cycling

Illegal in Venice itself though you'll see kids zooming around. Rent a bike on the Lido from Bruno Lazzari. ✪ *Gran Viale 21/B • Map H2*

3 Sailing

Yachtsmen gather at the marina on San Giorgio Maggiore island.

4 Swimming

Head for the Lido, or the crowded indoor pools at Sacca Fisola and Sant'Alvise. ✪ *Map C1*

5 In-line Skating

There is a small rink at Sant'Elena in Castello, otherwise stick to the Lido pavements *(see p115)*.

6 Golf

The well-reputed 18-hole course at the Alberoni is on the south of the Lido. ✪ *Map H2*

7 Tennis

The Lido has the only courts available to visitors. ✪ *Lungomare G Marconi 41/d • Map H2*

8 Jogging

The city's stone paving doesn't do wonders for your knees, so try the city parks.

9 Gyms

Private gyms with state-of-the-art equipment can be found in the *Yellow Pages*.

10 Football

The home team Venezia plays at Sant'Elena stadium most Sundays. ✪ *Map H2*

Left **Spizzico and Burger King** Centre **Feeding the pigeons in San Marco** Right **Ferry trip**

🔟 Places for Children

1 Play Areas
Children tired of art and architecture can release their energy at well-equipped playgrounds with slides, swings and frames at Parco Savorgnan near Ponte delle Guglie in Cannaregio and the fenced-in waterfront park at Giardini in Castello *(see p102)*. The vast shady green expanse of Sant'Elena even boasts a modest skating rink and an artificial climbing wall. Otherwise make friends with the city kids as they kick footballs or cycle around Campo San Polo *(see p81)* of an afternoon.

2 Ferry Trips
Restful for adults, exciting for youngsters, the varied boat lines are an ideal way for families to appreciate the joys of the city. Get older children to plan trips on the route maps but avoid the outside seating on the *vaporetto* with toddlers. For an extended trip, take the majestic double-decker *motonave* over to Lido and Punta Sabbioni *(see p135)*.

Glassmaking demonstration in Murano

3 Doge's Palace Prisons and Armoury
Children are thrilled by the spooky labyrinth of narrow passageways through the palace's erstwhile prisons, and it's fun deciphering the graffiti scratched on the walls by inmates over the centuries. In the armoury, hunt out the unusual child-sized suit from the 16th century, along with the protection for horses *(see pp12–15)*.

4 Museo Storico Navale
Easily the best city museum for children, this three-floor haven of shipbuilding includes Chinese junks and exhibits from World War II, such as the famed torpedoes guided by Italian Navy divers, responsible for sinking British warships *(see p41)*.

5 Museo di Storia Naturale
The star of the marvellous natural history museum is a 3.6-m (12-ft) tall and 7-m (23-ft) long skeleton of the dinosaur *Ouranosauris nigeriensis*, discovered in the Sahara Desert by the explorer Giancarlo Ligabue. Don't miss the new acquarium.
⊗ *Salizzada del Fondaco dei Turchi, S Croce 1730 • Map L1 • 041 275 02 06 • Open Sat–Sun 10am–4pm. Due to restructuring, some displays are temporarily closed. Free admission.*

6 Glassmaking Demonstrations
Magic moments are guaranteed as children are transfixed by skilful craftsmen blowing blobs

of molten glass into fine vases, or moulding coloured rods into myriad animal shapes. Small workshops are dotted all over Venice, while Murano has more large-scale furnaces – demonstrations are free, on the condition you stroll through the showroom afterwards *(see p109)*.

Spizzico and Burger King

A new and welcome introduction to Venice for families, for its indoor children's playground. This centrally located Italian-run hybrid hamburger, pizza and salad outlet has very reasonable prices and plentiful seating. ® *Campo S Luca, S Marco 4476 • Map P4 • 041 241 06 05*

Feeding the Pigeons

Scattering feed to the birds in Piazza San Marco *(see pp16–19)* while Mum and Dad immortalize you on video is a must for young visitors. Bags of corn are hawked by sellers, but the birds eat anything.

Laboratorio Blu Bookshop

Just off the main Cannaregio canal is this delightful bookshop dedicated to youngsters. One stand is packed with illustrated children's books in English, audio cassettes and games. Kids love crawling into the cubby hole to enjoy their purchases. ® *Ghetto Vecchio, Cannaregio 1224 • Map C1 • 041 715 819*

The Disney Store

Youngsters are greeted by Mickey Mouse on a bridge, while Donald Duck fishes an old boot out of a canal. Usual Disney fare is on sale. ® *Campo S Bartolomeo, S Marco 5257/98 • Map P3*

The Disney Store

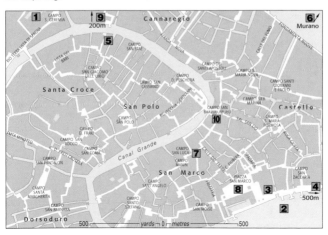

Left **La Fenice plaque** Centre **Malibran Theatre** Right **Goldoni Theatre**

🔟 Entertainment Venues

1 La Fenice
World-famous opera and concert performances are back at this glorious theatre, re-inaugurated in December 2003 *(see p73)*. Productions range from Verdi and Rossini to contemporary composers.
⊗ Tickets from Vela at Piazzale Roma or the theatre (041 2424) • Map N5 • www.teatrolafenice.it

2 Teatro Malibran
In a quiet square near Rialto stands the gleaming and splendid Malibran Theatre, re-inaugurated in 2001 to take on part of the Fenice's productions. Dating back to 1678 as Teatro Grimani, it was renamed after the 19th-century Spanish mezzo-soprano Maria Malibran.
⊗ Tickets as La Fenice • Corte del Teatro Malibran, Cannaregio • Map Q2

3 Films in English
The Giorgione cinema has English-language screenings one evening a week throughout the winter. In late summer, the outdoor cinema in Campo San

Venice Film Festival

Polo means delights from the Venice Film Festival.
⊗ Cinema Giorgione: Rio Terrà dei Franceschi, Cannaregio 4612 • Map E3• 041 522 62 98 • Venice Film Festival: 041 521 87 11 • www.labiennale.org

4 Teatro Goldoni
One of the oldest theatres in the city, dating from the 17th century. It acquired its present name in 1875 in honour of the 18th-century playwright Carlo Goldoni *(see p50)*. An excellent range of international plays is performed in Italian Nov–May. ⊗ Calle del Teatro, S Marco 4650/B • Map P4 • Ticket sales: 041 240 2014

5 Vivaldi Concerts
Inspiring performances of Vivaldi's music can be enjoyed just off Piazza San Marco. Tickets are available at agencies, hotels or directly from the palace. ⊗ Ateneo San Basso, Piazzetta dei Leoncini, San Marco • Map Q4 • 041 528 28 25 • www.vivaldi.it or www.virtuosidivenezia.com

6 Chamber Music
While listening to the uplifting notes of Vivaldi's *Four Seasons*, or a masterpiece from Bach or Benedetto Marcello take a moment to unwind and relax from the day's hectic sightseeing. The Church of San Vidal was rebuilt around 1700 and has a spacious interior. ⊗ Campo S. Vidal, S Marco 2944 • Map M6 • 041 277 05 61• www.interpretiveneziani.com

7 Concerts in Costume
Youthful but expert singers and musicians perform comic operas at the Scuola dei Carmini *(see p32)*. It makes for a memorable evening. ✆ *Scuola Grande dei Carmini, Campo S Margherita, Dorsoduro • Map J5 • 041 0994371 • www.veniceopera.it*

8 Ai Musicanti
The top-class orchestra and singers perform opera highlights by Verdi and Rossini, music by Vivaldi and Mozart, and Italian folk music. ✆ *Campo S Gallo, S Marco1092, • Map P5 • 041 520 89 22 • Closed Nov–Mar*

Teatro Fondamenta Nuove

9 Auditorium Santa Margherita
This converted cinema regularly stages live ethnic and other music – free! The programme is generally posted on the door. ✆ *Campo S Margherita, Dorsoduro 3689 • Map K5 • 041 234 99 11*

10 Teatro Fondamenta Nuove
Formerly a lumber store, since 1993 the premises have been buzzing with experimental theatre and contemporary dance. New tech music and off-beat films are also on the avant garde programme. ✆ *Fondamente Nuove, Cannaregio 5013 • Map E2 • 041 522 44 98 • www.teatrofondamentanuove.it*

Top 10 Films set in Venice

1 Indiana Jones and the Last Crusade (1989)
Hero Harrison Ford heaves up the floor in the church of San Barnaba.

2 Moonraker (1979)
Roger Moore as James Bond steers a gondola-cum-hovercraft across Piazza San Marco in a thrilling chase.

3 Death in Venice (1971)
Visconti's film starring Dirk Bogarde is now as classic as the Thomas Mann novel on which it is based *(see p51)*.

4 Don't Look Now (1973)
This thriller, with Donald Sutherland and Julie Christie, will keep you awake at night.

5 The Merchant of Venice (2004)
Starring Al Pacino as a brilliant Shylock.

6 Eve (1962)
Joseph Losey's black-and-white classic starring "temptress" Jeanne Moreau.

7 Senso (1954)
Alida Valli betrays family and country for an Austrian officer in another Visconti film.

8 Fellini's Casanova (1976)
Donald Sutherland walks around a fantasized version of Venice in this Fellini film.

9 Everyone Says I Love You (1996)
Woody Allen literally runs in to Julia Roberts as they both jog through the city.

10 The Wings of a Dove (1997)
Helena Bonham Carter stars in the film version of Henry James' Venetian story.

Left **Jesurum** Centre **Venini** Right **Nardi**

🔟 Shops in Venice

Mondonovo
Venice's most original *papier-mâché* masks. A monstrous bear's head might hang alongside a gloating Tutankhamun, but the speciality is Carnival costumes. Masks for the film *Eyes Wide Shut* (2000) were made here. ⊗ *Rio Terrà Canal, Dorsoduro 3063* • *Map C5*

Nardi
Elizabeth Taylor, Grace Kelly and Elton John have all happily spent time (and more) in this plush boutique of glittering marvels. Three generations of craftsmen have thrilled those who can afford it with breathtaking pieces, such as their blackamoor brooch in ruby and gold or diamond and platinum. ⊗ *Piazza S Marco 69, S Marco* • *Map Q5*

Jesurum
A triumphant showroom of exquisite lace and embroidery, founded in 1870. Ask to see the "back-up copy" of the delicate lace tablecloth commissioned by Queen Margherita which took 10 years to complete. The firm first acted as a trade school for poor girls. ⊗ *Piazza S Marco 60–1, S Marco* • *Map Q5*

Venini
Don't expect Venetian glass animals here, rather innovative platters and vases of great simplicity and style. Since its 1921 beginnings, Venini's award-winning design team has included top names Carlo Scarpa and Gae Aulenti. ⊗ *Piazzetta Leoncini, S Marco 314* • *Map Q4*

Perle e Dintorni
String together your own necklace in this great shop. Dazzling kaleidoscopic baubles range from traditional gay murrhine, to blown globes sprayed with gold and silver, Chinese ceramics and African bone beads. ⊗ *Calle della Mandola, S Marco 3740* • *Map N4*

Traditional Venetian masks on display in Mondonovo

For more on shopping in Venice See p138

Rizzo

Feel like jet-black tagliatelle ribbons made from cuttlefish ink for dinner? Or perhaps the blue Curaçao variety or the multi-coloured Carnival masks? These are only a taste of more than 40 imaginative pasta shapes by Rizzo – a marvellous souvenir.
◈ *Salizzada S Giovanni Grisostomo, Cannaregio 5778 • Map Q2*

Coin Department Store

It's impossible to walk past the stylishly dressed windows of Coin without being impressed. Centrally located close to the Rialto GPO, this branch of Italy's largest department chain has an elegant clothing range and sleekly designed homeware.
◈ *Salizzada S Giovanni Gristomo, Cannaregio 5785 • Map Q2*

Rubelli

Venice's past contact with the Orient is conjured up by the sumptuous handmade furnishings in this showroom. A blend of computer technology and traditional techniques is used for the brocades, damasks and silks.
◈ *Campiello del Teatro, S Marco 3877 • Map M4*

Paolo Olbi

Photo albums and address books in rainbow-coloured marbled paper and leather at reasonable prices, by one of the original craftsmen in Venice.
◈ *Calle della Mandola, S Marco 3653 • Map N4*

Venice Pavilion Bookshop

Excellent multilingual selection of literature and miscellany focusing on Venice. Also serves as a tourist information point and box office for cultural events.
◈ *Palazzetto Selva, Giardinetti Reali, S Marco 2 • Map Q5*

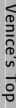

Top 10 Souvenirs

Glassware
Impress your guests back home with a genuine Murano chandelier or perhaps a *millefiori* paperweight.

Gourmet Food
For something authentically Italian but intrinsically Venetian, try extra virgin olive oil flavoured with chilli peppers, bottled red chicory paste or pasta in the shape of gondolas and masks.

T-shirts
The essential guaranteed souvenir of Venice, sold at the ubiquitous street stalls.

Masks
A mind-boggling array of masks, traditionally made for Carnival in *papier-mâché*, ceramic and even leather.

Marbled Paper
Swirls of pastel hues can be used for covering books or simply as elegant wrapping paper for gifts.

Beads
All manner of beads, from frosted glass, ceramic or the traditional colourful murrhine mosaic-style, can be found.

Italian Wine and Liqueurs
Take advantage of lower prices and taxes by stocking up on locally produced wines.

Fabric
Lace is the most Venetian of materials, but attractive linens and velvets are also good value.

Silverwork
Photo frames, letter openers and teaspoons make lovely gifts for friends.

Clothes
All the top fashion names can be found in Venice.

AROUND TOWN

VENICE'S TOP 10

Left **Busy streetlife in Campo San Bartolomeo** Right **Designer shopping on Mercerie**

San Marco

VENICE'S SMALLEST BUT FOREMOST *sestiere* *(district)* named after the city's patron saint is bounded by the Grand Canal on all but one side, which explains the number of stately palaces in the area. It revolves around the buzz of Piazza San Marco and the majestic Doge's Palace, the political and legal core of the city until the 18th century. Running off the square are the Mercerie and Calle Larga XXII Marzo, offering wall-to-wall designer shopping. But beyond that San Marco has a residential air, with a great range of places to eat. Don't hesitate to wander down minor alleyways: surprises include unusual wellheads and many craft workshops.

TOP 10 Sights

1. Piazza San Marco
2. Mercerie
3. Campo San Stefano
4. Teatro La Fenice
5. Scala Contarini del Bovolo
6. Campo San Bartolomeo
7. Chiesa di San Moisè
8. Palazzo Grassi
9. Museo Fortuny
10. Chiesa di Santa Maria del Giglio

Shop on the Mercerie

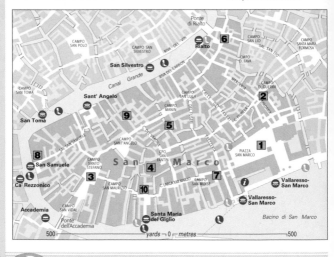

Piazza San Marco
See pp16–19.

Mercerie
The expensive elegance of Venice is most evident on this main thoroughfare linking Rialto and Piazza San Marco. *Mercerie* means haberdasher's, although these days it is the realm of the designer fashion outlets who are able to afford the sky-high rents. Just below the ornate Torre dell' Orologio archway is a sculpted female figure commemorating a housewife who lived here rent-free as a reward for inadvertently knocking a mortar into the street, killing a revolutionary leader and thus halting the short-lived Baiamonte Tiepolo revolt in 1310.
🖎 *Map Q4*

Campo San Stefano
This spacious, elegant square is edged by cafés with smart, white-jacketed waiters and colourful awnings. Its most regular inhabitants seem to be unhurried pigeons, pecking around the ornate lampposts, and local children at play watched over by nannies and doting grandparents. Pride of place in the centre goes to a statue of Niccolò Tommaseo, patriot and author of the *Risorgimento*. At Carnival time a lively outdoor craft market is held here, although it is not quite up to the level of merry-making seen here in olden times when there were magnificent balls and bull-fights. The latter events ended in 1802 when a stand collapsed on spectators.
🖎 *Map M5*

Teatro La Fenice
Long masked in scaffolding since a 1996 arson attack left it gutted, the historic "Phoenix" theatre has finally risen from the flames. Selva's 1792 opera house, just one of 17 theatres at the time, has staged countless world premieres including Rossini's *Tancredi* in 1813, five operas commissioned of Verdi, most notably *Rigoletto* and *La Traviata*, and more recent works by Stravinsky and Luigi Nono. Legendary divas Maria Callas and Dame Joan Sutherland have sung in this glorious setting.
🖎 *Campo S Fantin • Map N5 • See p66 • Daily guided tours*

Scala Contarini del Bovolo
Often used as a film set, this fine 15th-century palace with its beautiful external "snail-shell" staircase is squeezed into a diminutive square. Following careful restoration, visitors can now climb the winding steps via five floors of loggias to a dome sheltering a splendid belvedere. From here there are magical views over the city's rooftops.
🖎 *Corte dei Risi, S Marco 4299 • Map P4 • Open Apr–Oct: 10am–6pm daily; Nov–Mar: 10am–4pm Sat–Sun • Admission charge*

Antiques shop, Campo San Stefano

Glassmaking

Venetian glasswork exquisitely decorates chandeliers, chalices and mirrors and has long been in demand the world over, especially during the Golden Age of the 16th century. Although the industry moved to Murano in 1295 as a safety measure against fire decreed by the Great Council, many furnaces around the San Marco district welcome visitors.

Campo San Bartolomeo

The statue of celebrated Venetian playwright Carlo Goldoni scrutinizes the milling crowds on this crossroads square. Strategically placed for a host of inviting bars crammed into the alleys radiating off it, "San Bartolo" serves as the fashionable hang-out for the city's young and trendy. The northern end is occupied by the main post office, once home to Venice's German community *(see p53)*. They worshipped in the Chiesa di San Bartolomeo (open 10am–noon Tue, Thu & Sat; free admission). ✏ *Map P3*

Chiesa di San Moisè

So overloaded was the 1668 façade of this church with ostentatious Baroque stone decorations that several statues were removed in 1878 to save it from collapse. It has been blasted by critics as "the height of architectural folly" and by John Ruskin *(see p51)* as "one of the basest examples of the basest school of the Renaissance". Devoid of religious symbols, it is given over wholly to the glorification of the aristocratic Fini family, who laid out 30,000 ducats for the job. ✏ *Campo S Moisè, S Marco 4299 • Map P5 • Open 9:30am–12:30pm Mon–Sat • Free*

Palazzo Grassi

In 1985, the splendid salons of Palazzo Grassi were superbly restored under the supervision of leading architect Gae Aulenti. Set on the Grand Canal, the palace dates back to 1740 when a wealthy merchant family commissioned Giorgio Massari to design the building. It is located alongside the picturesque tree-shaded Campo San Samuele, which features a graceful Veneto-Byzantine bell tower. ✏ *S Samuele, S Marco 3231 • Map L5 • Open for exhibitions*

Museo Fortuny

Flamboyant Spanish artist and theatrical stage designer Mariano Fortuny y Madrazo (1871–1950) adopted Venice as his home and muse, and transformed this ponderous 15th-century palace in Gothic-Venetian style into an exotic atelier. Although restoration is on-going, a number of rooms are open for temporary exhibitions. In the near future visitors will be able to admire Fortuny's sumptuous velvets,

Palazzo Grassi façade

Chiesa di Santa Maria del Giglio

renowned the world over, his famous pleated silk dresses, lamps, paintings, a remarkable stage curtain and fascinating 19th-century photographs.
⊗ *Campo S Beneto, S Marco 3780*
• Map N4 • Open for special exhibitions during restoration • Admission charge

🔟 Chiesa di Santa Maria del Giglio

Opening on to a lovely square next to the Grand Canal, this church is a further example of Venetian Baroque extravagance. Commissioned by the Barbaro family, its façade exalts their generations of maritime and political triumphs, with crests, galleys and statues. Relief maps along the lower plinth depict Zara, Candia, Padua, Rome, Corfu and Spalato, the fortified cities where many family members had served. Works of art inside the church include Venice's only canvas by the Flemish artist Rubens, depicting a curvaceous Madonna and child. Tintoretto's contributions are the Evangelists adorning the doors of the organ.
⊗ *Campo S Maria del Giglio, S Marco 3231 • Map N6 • Open 10am–5pm Mon–Sat, 1–5pm Sun • Admission charge*

A Day in San Marco

Morning

⏱ Visit the **Doge's Palace** on Piazza San Marco first *(see pp12–15)*, arriving early to fit it in. Must-sees are the Sala del Senato, Sala del Maggior Consiglio, prisons and the Bridge of Sighs. Then take a break for coffee in the modern café in the palace's former stables and watch the gondolas glide past the glassed-in doorway.

Time your visit to **Basilica San Marco** *(see pp8–11)* for midday, to catch the mosaics illuminated by huge spotlights so they glitter to their utmost. The tiles were laid at angles to catch the light.

🍴 Lunch at **Harry's Bar**, as Hemingway's hero did in *Across the River and into the Trees*. Order the *carpaccio*, wafer thin slices of raw beef, invented here by Cipriani *(see p21)*.

Afternoon

🛍 The **Mercerie** *(see p73)* is shopper's heaven, packed with international high fashion stores from Benetton to Cartier, and classy souvenir glass and hand-crafted paper workshops. For yet more, cross over to Calle Larga XXII Marzo for designer delights such as **Bulgari** jewellery and **Frette** linens *(see p76)*.

Return to **Piazza San Marco** *(see pp16–19)* in time to enjoy the views over Venice and the lagoon from the Campanile at dusk. At ground level again, it's time for a Bellini apéritif at **Caffè Florian** *(see p17)* to watch the sun set over the façade of the basilica.

Around Town – San Marco

Left **Frette** Centre **Benetton** Right **Cartier**

⭐10 Designer Boutiques

Frette
Since 1860 Frette has been importing top-grade cotton from Egypt and transforming it into towels and custom-made household linen. ◈ *Calle Larga XXII Marzo, S Marco 2070/A • Map P5*

L'Isola – Carlo Moretti
Contemporary glass at its innovative best, exhibited in galleries all over the world. Moretti's trademarks are "paper cone" vases, tumblers and huge sculptures. ◈ *Campo S Moisè, S Marco 1468 • Map P5*

MA.RE
This delightful boutique stocks the divine Salviati glass creations. First and foremost are the delicately etched modern wine glasses. ◈ *Via XXII Marzo, S Marco 2088 • Map P5*

Benetton
The vibrant colours and simple styles of T-shirts, jackets and jeans attract buyers young and old to this internationally renowned clothes chain. This shop is located in spacious two-floor premises close to Rialto. ◈ *Via II Aprile, S Marco 5051/5056 • Map P3*

Epicentro
Alessi kettles, heart-shaped hot-water bottles, designer garlic presses – you'll find the perfect gift here for friends who think they have everything. ◈ *Calle dei Fabbri, S Marco 932 • Map P4*

Cartier
World-famous French jewellers whose fortress-like premises gleam with gold, precious stones, handbags and watches. ◈ *Mercerie S Zulian, S Marco 606 • Map Q4*

MaxMara
For more than 50 years this family company has been designing fashionable clothes and accessories for city girls. ◈ *Campo S Salvador, S Marco 5033 • Map P3*

Bulgari
Striking contemporary jewellery, watches, accessories and Rosenthal porcelain. ◈ *Calle Larga XXII Marzo, S Marco 2282 • Map P5*

Fratelli Rossetti
Superb Italian elegance from this 50-year-old family-run firm, known worldwide for shoes, belts, bags and jackets. ◈ *Campo S Salvador, S Marco 4800 • Map P3*

Fendi
Flamboyant frocks and shoes for special occasions and crazily beaded bags, all with the "double-F" Fendi mark. ◈ *S Moisè, S Marco 1474 • Map P5*

For more on shopping in Venice See p138

Left **Leon d'Oro** Centre **Legatoria Piazzesi** Right **Bevilacqua**

Craft Shops

1 Venetia Studium
Exquisite hanging silk lamps of Fortuny design are reproduced with hand-painted patterning and glass beading. ◎ *Calle Larga XXII Marzo, S Marco 2403–6 • Map P5*

2 Legatoria Piazzesi
The only people in Venice still printing paper with hand-cut blocks, as well as binding books. ◎ *Campiello della Feltrina, S Marco 2511 • Map N6*

3 Pagnacco
Polar bears, squirrels and kangaroos are but some of the 200 glass animals this wonderful shop boasts. Orchestras of tiny glass musicians fill the shop window. ◎ *Mercerie, S Marco 231 • Map Q4*

4 Leon d'Oro
Commedia dell'arte marionettes, musical puppet theatres and glittering carnival masks for sale or hire. ◎ *Frezzeria, S Marco 1770 • Map P5*

5 Galleria Livio De Marchi
Crumpled boots and a raincoat slung over a chair are actually sculptures – there are even life-size wooden cars, complete with engines. ◎ *Salizzada S Samuele, S Marco 3157/A • Map M5*

6 Rigattieri
Ceramic enthusiasts must not miss this extraordinary shop of beautiful pottery. ◎ *Calle dei Frati, S Marco 3535/36 • Map M5*

7 Valese Fonditore
The Valese family foundry has been creating animals, lamps and door knockers in brass and bronze since 1913. Examples of their work can be found in Buckingham Palace and The White House. ◎ *Calle Fiubera, S Marco 793 • Map Q4*

8 Bevilacqua
Velvet and silk cushions, tapestries and curtain tassels are a feast for the eyes. ◎ *Campo S Maria del Giglio, S Marco 2520 • Map N5*

9 Le Botteghe della Solidarità
A kaleidoscopic display of handwoven shawls from India and musical instruments from African countries are part of an enterprise to guarantee artisans a just income. ◎ *Salizzada Pio X, S Marco 5164 • Map P3*

10 Daniela Ghezzo Segalin a Venezia
As well as the brocade slippers and bizarre footwear with built-in toes, special order shoes are also crafted here. ◎ *Calle dei Fuseri, S Marco 4365 • Map P4*

Left **Devil's Forest Pub** Centre **Bar al Teatro** Right **Le Café**

🔟 Bars and Cafés

1 Pasticceria Zanin
The coffee and cake shop for Venetians. The narrow bar only does counter service, so you have to stand up for your *cappuccino* and croissant for breakfast or Campari soda in the evening. Delectable ice cream in summer. ✎ *Campo S Luca, S Marco 4589 • Map P4*

2 Pasticceria Marchini
No drinks or seating, but a paradise for those with a sweet tooth. Orange and pistachio chocolates come in Venetian mask shapes. ✎ *Spadaria, S Marco 676 • Map E4*

3 Caffè Brasilia
Tuck in to a huge fresh fruit salad smothered with yogurt or a *tramezzino* sandwich in this quiet side-alley café. The coffee's good too. ✎ *Calle dei Assassini, S Marco 3658 • Map N4*

4 Bar al Teatro
Next door to the renowned Fenice Theatre *(see p73)*, this legendary establishment offers outdoor seating on a patio. Otherwise go inside to the bar and munch a toasted sandwich. ✎ *Campo S Fantin, S Marco 1916 • Map N5*

5 Devil's Forest Pub
This "pub" sports a real red London phonebox, draught beers and ales, light meals served until midnight and even a dartboard and live music. ✎ *Calle dei Stagneri, S Marco 5185 • Map Q3*

6 Caffè al Ponte del Lovo
Venetian sweetmeats can be enjoyed here, but most come for the Spritz apéritif, reputedly the best in town *(see p57)*. ✎ *Ponte dell'Ovo, S Marco 4819 • Map P4*

7 Le Café
Have a fresh orange juice or a *cappuccino* and pastry as you watch life go by in the square. ✎ *Campo S Stefano, S Marco 2797 • Map M5*

8 Hostaria ai Rusteghi
Excellent wines from Friuli, Tuscany and the Veneto, served with delectable, savoury titbits. ✎ *Campiello del Tentor, S Marco 5513 • Map P3*

9 McDonald's
Burgers and French fries at approachable prices, though the decor is the same the world over. ✎ *Calle Larga S Marco 656 • Map Q4*

10 Ai Assassini
A great *osteria* in a cul-de-sac near the Fenice. Stand at the bar for appetizing snacks or treat yourself to a table. ✎ *Rio Terrà dei Assassini, S Marco 3695 • Map N4*

For more Venice wine bars See pp56–7

Left **Ristorante all'Angelo** Right **Rosticceria San Bartolomeo**

TOP 10 Places to Eat

1 Hostaria à Masaniello
Marvellous southern Italian eatery. The menu includes buffalo mozzarella shipped daily from Naples. ⊗ *Campo S Stefano, S Marco 2801 • Map M5 • 041 520 90 03 • Closed Tue, mid-Nov–mid-Dec • €€€€*

2 Ristorante alla Borsa
A great selection of wines accompany dishes such as clams, mussels, tomatoes and capers. ⊗ *Calle delle Veste, S Marco 2018 • Map N6 • 041 523 54 34 • Closed Wed • €€€€*

3 Ristorante all'Angelo
A long-running favourite with seating for 680. Try the *risotto di seppie* (rice cooked with cuttlefish black ink sauce). ⊗ *Calle Larga S Marco, S Marco 403 • Map Q4 • 041 520 92 99 • €€€*

4 Rosticceria San Bartolomeo
Try the local favourite here, *mozzarella in carozza*, a deep-fried cheese sandwich. ⊗ *Calle della Bissa, S Marco 5424 • Map P3 • 041 522 35 69 • No disabled access • €*

5 Chat qui rit
Self-service restaurant with generous plates of pasta and salads served inside or out. ⊗ *Calle Tron, S Marco 1131 • Map P5 • 041 522 90 86 • Closed Sat & 2 weeks Jan • €*

6 Leon Bianco
Great for a cheap lunch of *pasta e fagioli* (bean and pasta soup) or lasagne, at the bar or at a table outside. ⊗ *Campo S Luca, S Marco 4153 • Map P4 • 041 522 11 80 • No credit cards • Closed Sat & Sun • €*

7 Al Bacareto
A 30-year institution. Try the *bigoli in salsa* (spaghetti with anchovy and onion purée). Outdoor seating. ⊗ *Calle delle Botteghe, S Marco 3447 • Map M5 • 041 528 93 36 • Closed Sun, Aug • €*

8 Al Vaporetto
Spacious self-service eatery. Choice of hot meals, pizza or rolls. ⊗ *Calle della Mandola, S Marco 3726 • Map N4 • 041 522 94 98 • Closed Mon & Jan • €*

9 La Caravella
Resembling a caravel sailing ship, the trestle tables are adorned with pewter plates. Fish and meat dishes. Good wine list. ⊗ *Via XXII Marzo, S Marco 2398 • Map P5 • 041 520 89 01 • No disabled access • €€€€€*

10 Acqua Pazza
Mediterranean cuisine, including Neapolitan-style pizza. ⊗ *Campo Sant'Angelo, S Marco 3808/10 • Map N5 • 041 277 06 88 • Closed Mon, Jan • No disabled access • €€€€*

Price Categories

For a three-course meal for one with half a bottle of wine (or equivalent meal), taxes and extra charges.	€ under €30
	€€ €30–€40
	€€€ €40–€50
	€€€€ €50–€60
	€€€€€ over €60

Note: *Unless otherwise stated, all restaurants accept credit cards and serve vegetarian meals*

Left **Scuola Grande di San Rocco** Right **Campo San Giacomo dell'Orio**

San Polo and Santa Croce

VENICE'S GREATEST CONCENTRATION *of sights can be found in these neighbouring districts, at the geographical heart of Venice, having grown up* around the ancient core of Rialto where the first inhabitants settled. Here, glorious churches, landmark monuments and breathtaking palaces are all saturated in history. Essential sights include Santa Maria Gloriosa dei Frari, the Scuola Grande di San Rocco where Tintoretto demonstrated his genius on sumptuous canvases, and the morning bustle of Rialto market. The squares of San Polo and San Giacomo dell'Orio are both full of cafés and benches for resting weary feet.

Sights

1. Rialto Market
2. Campo San Polo
3. Scuola Grande di San Rocco
4. Campo San Giacomo dell'Orio
5. Chiesa di San Giacomo dell'Orio
6. Scuola Grande di San Giovanni Evangelista
7. Palazzo Mocenigo
8. Giardino Papadopoli
9. Campo San Zan Degolà
10. Ca' Pesaro Museo di Arte Orientale

Interior detail, Scuola Grande di San Rocco

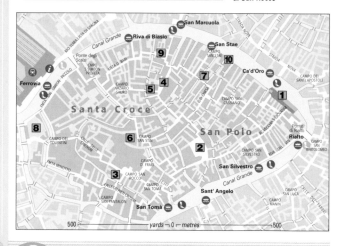

Rialto Market
See pp28–9.

Campo San Polo
This lovely square undergoes a series of transformations, from attractive theatre or dance area during Carnival, to open-air cinema through the summer months, and playground for bicycle- and scooter-mad kids the rest of the year. It has never been particularly quiet – it was once a venue for bullfights and bird-netting, extravagant parties with fireworks displays and even crime. In 1548 Florentine writer in hiding Lorenzino de' Medici was stabbed to death here on orders from the great Cosimo de' Medici. It was punishment for the assassination of Cosimo's cousin Duke Alessandro, which brought the Medici line to an end. ◎ *Map M3*

Scuola Grande di San Rocco
Blinding in the morning sun thanks to its cleansing face-lift, the early Renaissance façade of this historic building, home to masterpieces by Tintoretto, is a marvel of intertwined sculpted stone wreaths and crouching elephants dwarfed by admirable columns. The Istrian stone facing is embedded with a rainbow medley of burgundy porphyry and green and cream veined marble inserts. Designed by Bartolomeo Bon in 1517 and added to by Scarpagnino and other stone-masons, the imposing building with neighbouring church was home to one of the city's foremost confraternities, honoured with an annual visit by the Doge. ◎ *Campo S Rocco, S Polo 2454 ● Map K4 ● Open Apr–Oct: 9am–5:30pm daily; Nov–Mar: 10am–4pm daily (closed 25 Dec, 1 Jan, Easter Sun) ● Admission charge*

Campo San Giacomo dell'Orio
Named after either a bay tree, wolves or a canal depending on your source, this picturesque quintessential square, well off the beaten track, sports plane trees, benches for relaxing and patches of grass. Modest surrounding palaces are home to Venice University's architectural faculties. The laid-back air and abundance of eateries and coffee shops make it very inviting, and there's no lack of subjects for photographers or artists. ◎ *Map L2*

Chiesa di San Giacomo dell'Orio
On no account miss this unusual church. Founded in the 9th century, its Latin-cross shape boasts a marvellous 15th-century wood-beamed ceiling and a forest of colourful granite and black limestone columns from the Middle East, several of them loot from the Crusades. The floor merits close scrutiny for its multitude of fossils, while memorable paintings include Palma

Chiesa di San Rocco

Scuole

The Venetian *Scuole* (literally "schools") were charitable institutions of medieval origin, almost Masonic in organisation. Some were religious-orientated lay confraternities while others functioned as trade guilds. Up to 500 once operated, covering everyone from sausage-makers to cobblers. Several have survived, namely San Rocco and Carmini.

il Giovane's *Descent of Manna* (1580–81), left of the main altar, and a painted crucifix (1350) attributed to Paolo Veneziano.
Ⓢ Campo S Giacomo dell'Orio, S Croce
• Map L2 • Open 10am–5pm Mon–Sat, 1–5pm Sun • Admission charge

6 Scuola Grande di San Giovanni Evangelista

This erstwhile confraternity headquarters with a high-ceilinged upstairs hall is mostly used for conferences. The monumental staircase was the work of Coducci and the priceless reliquary contains a fragment of the True Cross, presented to the Scuola in 1369. The spectacular *Miracles of the Cross* cycle of paintings commissioned of Gentile Bellini and associates is now in the Accademia Galleries *(see pp24–5)*. The exterior courtyard has a fine sculptured portal screen by Pietro Lombardo mounted with an eagle to symbolize St John. Ⓢ Campiello della Scuola, S Polo 2454 • Map L3 • 041 71 82 34 phone to arrange an appointment

Scuola Grande di San Giovanni Evangelista

7 Palazzo Mocenigo

An 18th-century patrician palace whose richly furnished and frescoed rooms also have showcases of historic fabrics and costumes including lavishly embroidered waistcoats, fans, bodices and corsets. The Mocenigo family portrait gallery boasts a total of seven doges, topped in fame by Alvise I, the victor at the 1571 Battle of Lepanto against the Turks, which was crucial for the Republic.
Ⓢ Salizzada S Stae, S Croce 1992
• Map M2 • Open Apr–Oct: 10am–5pm Tue–Sun; Nov–Mar: 10am–4pm Tue–Sun
• Admission charge

Giardino Papadopoli

8 Giardino Papadopoli

A leafy haven of twittering sparrows and flowerbeds close to Piazzale Roma and the car parks, these French-designed gardens date back to the 1800s when extravagant parties for the nobility were held here among exotic flowers and rare animals. Site of a demolished convent, it belonged to Corfu-born entrepreneurs, hence the Greek

Campo San Zan Degolà

name. The public park was greatly reduced in size when the Rio Novo canal was excavated 1932–3. Ⓢ *Map J3*

9 Campo San Zan Degolà

People usually hurry through this square en route to the bus terminal, oblivious to its quiet charm. Interest starts with the curious loggia on the western canal edge, then there's the attractive plain church named for San Giovanni Decollato or St John the Beheaded, depicted with flowing curly locks in a stone *bas-relief* on the southern wall. Inside the simple Veneto-Byzantine building are lovely 13th-century frescoes, an unusual survivor for damp old Venice. Ⓢ *Map L1 • Chiesa di San Giovanni Decollato: open 10am–noon Mon–Sat*

10 Ca' Pesaro Museo di Arte Orientale

This impressive Oriental Art Collection is an eclectic mix of 19th-century curiosities from all over the Far East. Exhibits include armour, porcelain and costumes, dainty lacquerwork boxes and musical instruments. The neighbouring modern art gallery in monumental Ca' Pesaro *(see p20 and p41)* has also recently re-opened after restructuring. Ⓢ *Fondamenta Pesaro, S Croce 2076 • Map N1 • Open 10am–6pm (until 5pm in winter), closed public hols • Admission charge*

A Day in San Polo

Morning

Drink your fill of Tintoretto's dynamic paintings at the **Scuola Grande di San Rocco** *(see p81)* before wandering east to **Campo San Polo** *(see p81)*. Coffee is a must in the square, either at one of the local bars or at the attractive **Antica Birraria La Corte** *(see p85)*.

It's not far from here to **Rialto Market** *(see pp28–9)* for late morning bargains of fresh produce, often nearing half price when stall-holders are in a hurry to shut up shop. If this has worked up an appetite, a Grand Canal-side lunch is worth consideration at this point. There is a string of eateries spread along the sun-blessed Riva del Vin, close to the foot of Rialto Bridge. Each displays live lobster and fish and multi-lingual menus. In winter diners sit in see-through "tents" so that views of the canal and the procession of boats are ensured.

Afternoon

Make your way north and explore the craft and gift shops, lace, scarf and T-shirt stalls along Ruga Rialto and the old red-light area of **Rio Terrà Rampani** *(see p48)*.

Try to end up in pretty **Campo San Giacomo dell'Orio** *(see p81)* for a pre-dinner drink at Al Prosecco wine bar *(Campo S Giacomo dell'Orio, S Croce 1503 • 041 524 02 22 • Closed Sun)*. Ask for the fruity red Refosco from Friuli and *bocconcino con mortadella di cinghiale* (bite-sized roll with wild boar slice).

Left **Gilberto Penzo** Centre **Sabbie e Nebbie** Right **Hibiscus**

Craft Shops

1 Gilberto Penzo
A visit to this workshop with beautiful wooden models of traditional Venetian boats is a real treat. Many craft come in DIY kit form. ◈ *Calle II° dei Saoneri, S Polo 2702 • Map M3*

2 Mazzon le Borse
For 50 years Papa Piero has been personally making beautiful leather bags that last a lifetime. Luckily his daughter Marta is taking over the reins. ◈ *Campiello S Tomà, S Polo 2807 • Map L4*

3 Tragicomica
The result of 20 years of creating elaborate *papier-mâché* and leather masks and brocade costumes for Carnival as well as theatrical productions can be appreciated in this spectacular craft shop where the staff explain the significance of pieces. ◈ *Calle dei Nomboli, S Polo 2800 • Map M4*

4 Rivoaltus
Beautiful hand-bound diaries and address books can be purchased from this tiny shop right on the Rialto bridge. ◈ *Ponte di Rialto, S Polo 11 • Map P3*

5 Michele Cicogna
Looking for a Blackamoor lampstand, gilded cherub or a dresser adorned with Canaletto-style scenes? This vast show-room akin to a museum is the workshop of a skilled restorer. ◈ *Campo S Tomà, S Polo 2867 • Map L4*

6 La Pedrera
Handmade beads, photo frames and Murano glass creations. ◈ *Campo Sant'Agostin, S Polo 2279/b • Map L3*

7 Sabbie e Nebbie
Tasteful boutique of pottery, candles and oddities from Japan and Italy. ◈ *Calle dei Nomboli, S Polo 2768/a • Map M4*

8 Attombri
In an old covered passageway long home to the Rialto Market goldsmiths is a young designer who makes limited-edition necklaces. ◈ *Sottoportego degli Orefici, S Polo 74 • Map P2*

9 Hibiscus
A mix of Indian silk jackets, platters from Morocco and ceramic bowls by a Veneto artisan. ◈ *Ruga Rialto, S Polo 1060/61 • Map P2*

10 La Margherita Ceramica
Egg cups, teapots and platters are some of the delightful hand-turned objects available here. ◈ *Sottoportego de la Siona Bettina, S Croce 2345 • Map N2*

For what to buy in Venice **See p69**

Price Categories

For a three-course meal for one with half a bottle of wine (or equivalent meal), taxes and extra charges

€ under €30
€€ €30–€40
€€€ €40–€50
€€€€ €50–€60
€€€€€ over €60

Left **Il Réfolo** Right **Taverna Da Baffo sign**

Places to Eat

1 La Zucca
Delicious vegetarian fare, with the promise of unforgettable chocolate desserts. ◈ *Ponte del Megio, S Croce 1762 • Map L1 • 041 524 1570 • Closed Sun • No disabled access • €€*

2 Il Réfolo
Non-smoking gourmet pizzeria in a beautiful setting alongside a church and canal. ◈ *Campo del Piovan, S Croce 1459 • Map L2 • 041 524 0016 • No disabled access • Closed Mon, Tue L, Nov–Apr • €*

3 Al Nono Risorto
Lively eatery with youthful clientele and great pizzas served in the garden. ◈ *Sottoportego de la Siora Bettina, S Croce 2337 • Map N2 • 041 524 1169 • Closed Wed, Thu L • No credit cards • No disabled access • €€*

4 Al Ponte
Canalside setting and home-style Venetian cooking, such as *polpette* (meatballs). ◈ *Calle Larga San Giacomo dell'Orio, S Croce 1666 • Map L2 • 041 719 777 • Closed Sun • €*

5 Ai Coghi
Grilled meat and veg, along with pizza and fish. ◈ *Rio Terà S Silvestro, S Polo 1022/A • Map N3 • 041 522 7307 • €€*

6 Frary's
A welcoming eatery whose menu features flavours from the Middle East. ◈ *Fondamenta dei Frari, S Polo 2559 • Map L3 • 041 720 050 • Closed Tue • No disabled access • €*

7 Antica Birraria La Corte
Delectable pizzas named after the city's bridges feature at this ultra-modern eatery set in a former brewery. There is also a pleasant, tree-shaded patio. ◈ *Campo S Polo, S Polo 2168 • Map M3 • 041 275 0570 • €*

8 Gelateria Alaska
Unforgettable ice cream made by a true maestro, Carlo. This is the real deal – 100 per cent natural *gelato* with ginger, spearmint, pistachio, rose petals and green tea! ◈ *Calle Larga dei Bari, S Croce 1159 • Map K2 • €*

9 Taverna Da Baffo
Seek out this tranquil square for a light lunch with a glass of Belgian beer or crisp Friuli wine. ◈ *Campo della Chiesa, S Polo 2346 • Map L3 • 041 520 8862 • €*

10 Pasticceria Targa
Delicious thick hot chocolate goes down well with a *zaeto* or *moretto*, traditional Italian biscuits, or any of the tasty pastries. ◈ *Rughetta del Ravano, S Polo 1080 • Map N3 • €*

Note: *Unless otherwise stated, all restaurants accept credit cards and serve vegetarian meals*

Left **Zattere** Right **Squero di San Trovaso**

Dorsoduro

A DISTRICT OF CONTRASTS, *Dorsoduro stretches from the port, backed by an historic but rather run-down zone long home to sailors and fishermen, via the panoramic Zattere and Grand Canal, all the way to the Punta della Dogana, a chic area of foreign consulates and wealthy residences. Highlights for visitors include two foremost art galleries, the Accademia and the Peggy Guggenheim Collection, crammed with masterpieces ancient and modern, as well as Ca' Rezzonico palace and magnificent churches, Santa Maria della Salute and San Sebastiano, the latter famous for its wonderful Veronese canvases. Literally the "hard backbone" of Venice as it was built on elevated islands of compacted subsoil, Dorsoduro used to be sparsely populated due to its exposure to pirate attacks. Today, as home to most of the city's university premises, it is full of lively cafés, bars and nightlife, concentrated in the market square, Campo Santa Margherita.*

🔟 Sights

1	Accademia Galleries	6	Rio Terrà dei Catecumeni
2	Zattere	7	Ex Ospedale degli Incurabili
3	San Nicolò dei Mendicoli	8	Campo San Barnaba
4	Squero di San Trovaso	9	Chiesa dei Gesuati
5	Chiesa di San Sebastiano	10	San Basilio Port Zone

San Nicolò dei Mendicoli

Preceding pages **The domes of San Marco**

Accademia Galleries
See pp24–5.

Zattere
This broad waterfront took its name from the rafts of timber (zattere) floated downstream from the extensive forests in the northern Dolomite region which were managed by the Venetian Republic. The precious wood was used for constructing palaces or transformed into masts and the like for the important shipbuilding industry. The tall-masted sailing ships and rowing boats which used to moor here have been replaced by motorized vaporetti and tourist launches, and nowadays the Zattere signifies lovely lagoon views, perfect for a day or evening stroll. ◈ Map C5

San Nicolò dei Mendicoli
This Veneto-Byzantine church with an imposing square campanile (bell tower) will be recognized by film buffs from the chilling Nicholas Roeg film Don't Look Now. Hidden away in a maze of narrow alleyways off the port zone, "St Nicholas of the beggars" has a pretty portico which doubled as a shelter for the poor. Founded in the 7th century, it is the second oldest church in Venice. In the 1970s it was restored by the Venice in Peril Fund, who water-proofed the low floor.
◈ Campo S Nicolò, Dorsoduro 1907 • Map A5 • 041 275 03 82 • Open 10am–noon, 4–6pm Mon–Sat • Free

Squero di San Trovaso
This is by far the city's most famous gondola repair and construction yard, though its active days may be numbered. The combined workshop-dwelling, its window sills clad with geraniums, is reminiscent of an Alpine chalet as the first occupants came from the mountainous Cadore region. Though closed to visitors, it backs on to a canal (Rio di San Gervasio e Protasio) so it's easy to watch the goings-on as oar-propelled craft are brought in for caulking and cleaning. ◈ Map C5

Chiesa di San Sebastiano
This 16th-century church is a treasure trove of Paolo Veronese paintings, and the artist devoted most of his life to the specta-cular fresco cycle (see p39).
◈ Campo S Sebastiano, Dorsoduro 1907 • Map B5 • 041 275 04 62 • Open 10am–5pm Mon–Sat, 1–5pm Sun • Admission charge

Rio Terrà dei Catecumeni
This reclaimed thoroughfare between the Zattere and Santa Maria della Salute is dominated by a long building, now a school, where prisoners-of-war of the Republic who did not profess the Christian faith would be held captive until they converted. This quiet backwater comes alive on 21 November when the Salute festivities are in full swing (see p63). ◈ Map D5

Ex Ospedale degli Incurabili façade

Boats moored at the San Basilio Port Zone

7 Ex Ospedale degli Incurabili

A cavernous, labyrinthine construction that takes up a lengthy stretch of the Zattere, this erstwhile hospital has undergone vast renovations to adapt it for the Accademia Art Institute, which has transferred here to leave the historic galleries room for expansion *(see pp24–5)*. The building dates from the 1500s, founded to shelter women with incurable venereal diseases, and later took in orphans and a trade school. Legend has it that St Francis Xavier, ordained in Venice, was sent to serve here with his companions on orders from Ignatius Loyola. More recently, it has served as a juvenile court. ✎ *423 Zettere, Dorsoduro 30135 • Map C5 • Closed to public*

8 Campo San Barnaba

Nowadays a modest square dotted with some low-key bars, its main attraction is a colourful moored barge loaded high with shiny fresh fruit and vegetables – a must for photographers. Its history has not always been so peaceful, however – the square used to be the arena for fierce rivalries between the city's working class bands, the Nicolotti and Castellani, who would fight it out on the Ponte dei Pugni *(see p47)*. On a more forgiving note, the rather nondescript church used to take in disgraced and bankrupt nobility. ✎ *Map K5*

9 Chiesa dei Gesuati

Set right on the Zattere waterfront close to the main ferry moorings, the Gesuati (also known as Santa Maria del Rosario) is often confused with the Gesuiti (Jesuit) establishment in Cannaregio. Taking over from a minor religious order, the Domenican friars had this church

---

Masks

Handmade in *papier-mâché* and glittery plaster, Venetian masks are now strictly tourist fare, but they were once essential attire during Carnival, allowing aristocrats to enjoy themselves in anonymity. One unusual model, with a long curved nose, was used by doctors during plagues, its cavity filled with perfumed herbs to filter the diseased air.

constructed in Classical style in 1726 by Giorgio Massari. Inside the ceiling consists of three uplifting frescoes (1737–9) by Tiepolo (see p44), which are considered among his best work, portraying St Dominic amid glorious angels in flight. ✧ *Fondamente delle Zattere, Dorsoduro 864 • Map C5 • Open 10am–5pm Mon–Sat, 1–5pm Sun • Admission charge*

San Basilio Port Zone
The vast docks occupy a good part of the northwestern continuation of the Zattere waterfront, and are usually crowded with trucks and cars queueing up to board the ferries to Greece. The modern terminal also handles the increasing cruise liner traffic, whereas the former industrial structures such as the cotton mill and cold stores are being converted for use by Venice University (see p54). The outstanding 17th-century pastel portrait artist Rosalba Carriera (see p25) was born in the San Basilio parish and returned there to die, destitute and totally blind, in 1757. ✧ *Map B5*

Statue in Chiesa dei Gesuati

Exploring Dorsoduro

Morning

The **Accademia Galleries** (see pp24–5) can be overwhelming, so focus on a selection of its glories, but don't neglect the Carpaccios and Bellinis. After all that art, have a relaxing coffee watching the boats go by at Snack Bar Accademia Foscarini, a magical spot right at the foot of Accademia Bridge. (Rio Terrà Antonio Foscarini, Dorsoduro 878/C • 041 522 72 81 • Closed Tue).

Next, head off east for a leisurely stroll, past Longhena's work of art, the church of **Santa Maria della Salute** (see p38), to Punta della Dogana, a great spot for taking photos of Piazza San Marco. Turn back in the direction of the Zattere and Giudecca Canal. Lunch is recommended at Al Chioschetto, a snack bar right on the water's edge. (Zattere, Dorsoduro 1406/a).

Afternoon

Wander through to **Campo Santa Margherita** (see pp32–3) to the Scuola Grande dei Carmini to admire Tiepolo's canvases, then take time to admire the architectural curiosities of this fascinating square.

As sunset approaches waste no time in occupying a table for a Spritz apéritif at the trendy bar Margaret DuChamp (Campo S Margherita, Dorsoduro 3019 • 041 528 62 55 • Closed Tue). It's hard to better this as a place for people-watching, and an added bonus is the scent of jasmine that fills the air as night falls.

Left **BAC Art Studio** Right **Totem-II Canale Gallery sign**

Shops

1 869
Paola Carraro transforms paintings by modern masters Klee, Magritte and others into hand-knitted sweaters and dresses. Commissions are taken so you can wear your favourite painting. ◈ *Piscina del Forner, Dorsoduro 869 • Map D5*

2 Bac Art Studio
Attractive and affordable etchings and prints of Venice by artists Baruffaldi and Cadore. Buy them framed if desired. ◈ *Piscina del Forner, Dorsoduro 862 • Map D5*

3 Totem-II Canale Gallery
Bulky ancient beads, made with vitreous paste and once traded in Africa, are now precious antiques. Contemporary African wood artworks as well. ◈ *Rio Terrà Antonio Foscarini, Dorsoduro 878/B • Map C5*

4 Signor Blum
Detailed jigsaw models of Gothic palaces, flanked by wall panels and painted toy figures all individually handmade by this co-operative of female artisans. ◈ *Campo S Barnaba, Dorsoduro 2840 • Map K5*

5 Augusto Mazzon
Everyone's Christmas tree needs one of the joyous gilded cherubs lovingly crafted by wood-carver and painter Danilo. He also makes picture frames and furniture. ◈ *Calle del Traghetto, Dorsoduro 2783 • Map L5*

6 Laboratorio Fustat
Stunning ceramics made on the spot by talented Cinzia, who also runs pottery courses here. ◈ *Campo S Margherita, Dorsoduro 2904 • Map K5 • 335 604 56 75*

7 Ca' Macana
Mask-makers extraordinaire, with life-size unicorns, pointy jester heads with bells and the full Carnival range. ◈ *Calle delle Botteghe, Dorsoduro 3172 • Map L5*

8 Billa Supermarket
Open seven days a week with freshly baked bread, great cheese and salami counter, wine, fruit and vegetables. ◈ *Zattere, Dorsoduro 1491 • Map B5*

9 Il Mondo in Miniatura
Miniatures of Venice's palaces and bridges modelled by the craftsman who has produced a 6 x 4m (20 x 13 ft) model of the entire city. ◈ *Calle della Toletta, Dorsoduro 1193 • Map L6*

10 Arras
Original hand-woven fabrics, garments and bags in beautiful colours. ◈ *Campiello Squelini, Dorsoduro 3235 • Map L5*

For more on shopping in Venice See p138

Price Categories

For a three-course	€ under €30
meal for one with half	€€ €30–€40
a bottle of wine (or	€€€ €40–€50
equivalent meal), taxes	€€€€ €50–€60
and extra charges	€€€€€ over €60

Left **Gelateria Nico** Right **La Rivista**

🔟 Places to Eat

1 Gelateria Nico
Venice's most renowned ice cream parlour. The local favourite is *giandiuotto da passeggio* – hazelnut and chocolate ice cream smothered in whipped cream. ◎ *Zattere, Dorsoduro 922 • Map C5 • 041 522 5293 • Closed Thu in winter • €*

2 Alla Toletta
Choose from an innovative range of pizza slices to take away, including wild mushroom, smoked ham, tomatoes and rocket. ◎ *Calle della Toletta, Dorsoduro 1309 • Map L6 • 041 523 6518 • €*

3 Pizzeria ai Sportivi
Easily the best pizza in Venice, with delicious toppings of Treviso radicchio or porcini mushrooms. Outdoor seating. ◎ *Campo S Margherita, Dorsoduro 3052 • Map K5 • 041 521 1598 • Closed Mon • €*

4 Bar Abbazia
Shaded by a leafy pergola, the outside tables are perfect for enjoying a quick sandwich. ◎ *Rio Terrà dei Catecumeni, Dorsoduro 128-129/A • Map D5 • 041 523 2149 • €*

5 Osteria da Codroma
This timber-panelled *osteria* enjoys a quiet and laid-back atmosphere. ◎ *Fondamenta Briati, Dorsoduro 2340 • Map B4 • 041 524 6789 • Closed Sun • €*

6 La Rivista
Innovative Italian cuisine in relaxing, designer modern surrounds. Inspiring choice of cheese and wines. ◎ *Rio Terrà Foscarini, Dorsoduro 979/a • Map C5 • 041 240 1425 • Closed Mon • €€€€*

7 Suzie Café
This great bar, frequented by students, serves sandwiches, pasta and salads. ◎ *Campo S Basilio, Dorsoduro 1527 • Map B5 • 041 522 7502 • Closed Sun in winter • €*

8 Ai Gondolieri
One of the city's top restaurants, specializing in game from the Veneto when in season. Extensive wine list. ◎ *Ponte del Formager, Dorsoduro 366 • Map D5 • 041 528 6396 • Closed Tue, Jul–Aug lunch • €€€€*

9 Pasticceria Tonolo
One of the city's best pastry shops. Delicious, freshly baked almond biscuits and mini pizzas are recommended. ◎ *Crosera S Pantalon, Dorsoduro 3764 • Map K4 • 041 523 7209 • Closed Mon • €*

10 Gelateria Il Doge
Try *Zuppa del doge* (candied fruit, egg custard and sponge cake soaked in Marsala) at this great ice cream parlour. ◎ *Campo S Margherita, Dorsoduro 3058A • Map K5 • 041 523 4607 • Closed Dec–Jan • €*

Note: *Unless otherwise stated, all restaurants accept credit cards and serve vegetarian meals*

Left **La Cantina** Right **Fondamenta degli Ormesini**

Cannaregio

ACCOUNTING FOR THE HUGE CRESCENT between the northern bank of the Grand Canal and the lagoon, the bustling sestiere of Cannaregio reaches from the railway station to the city hospital. It was home to Marco Polo and artists Titian and Tintoretto, and boasts landmark churches such as Madonna dell'Orto along with an old Jewish Ghetto. Named after the reeds (canne) that once filled its marshes, it is crossed by Strada Nova, the city's main thoroughfare, but also boasts Venice's narrowest alley, the 58-cm (2-ft) wide Calle Varisco. Never a dull moment passes thanks to its market, craft workshops and rowing clubs, while relaxation comes at the string of shady parks and laid-back cafés and bars that line the maze of back-street canals.

🔟 Top 10 Sights

1. Ca' d'Oro
2. Jewish Ghetto
3. Corte Seconda del Milion
4. Santa Maria dei Miracoli
5. Campo dei Mori
6. Farmacia Ponci
7. Fondamente della Misericordia and degli Ormesini
8. Palazzo Labia
9. Chiesa di San Giobbe
10. Fondamente Nuove

Chiesa di San Giobbe

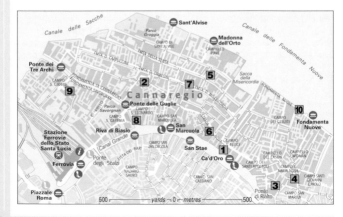

Ca' d'Oro

Behind the palace's beautiful Gothic tracery is a memorable column-filled courtyard paved with myriad coloured *tesserae*. Inside is the Galleria Franchetti, an enticing collection of paintings, sculptures, coins and ceramics donated to the State by Baron Giorgio Franchetti in 1916, together with the building. One highlight is Andrea Mantegna's agonizing *St Sebastian* (1560) pierced by arrows "like a hedgehog", in the portico leading through to a stunning loggia overlooking the Grand Canal. An ornate 15th-century staircase climbs to the second floor where there are huge 16th-century Flemish tapestries *(see p42)*. ◈ Calle Ca' d'Oro, Cannaregio 3932 • Map N1 • Open 8:15am–2pm Mon, 8:15am–7:15pm Tue–Sun • No disabled access • Admission charge

Jewish Ghetto

The word "ghetto" originated in Venice, derived from *getto* (casting) due to an old iron foundry here. As of 1492 many Jewish refugees reached Venice after expulsion from Spain and in 1527 they were obliged by law to move to this area. Subject to a curfew to prevent their fraternizing with local women, they slept behind locked gates, their island circled by an armed patrol boat. Waves of arrivals saw each language group build its own synagogue (five in all) and raise the low-ceilinged buildings to seven floors in height. Today 33 Jews still live in the ghetto, while a further 450 reside in other parts of the city. The synagogues can be visited with a guide and there's a museum of sacred objects. ◈ Museo Ebraico, Campo del Ghetto Nuovo, Cannaregio 2902/b • Map C1 • Open Jun–Sep: 10am–7pm Sun–Fri; Oct–May: 10am–6pm Sun–Fri • Admission charge

Moor sculpture

Corte Seconda del Milion

The newly restructured Malibran Theatre in this photogenic square was erected on the site of the Polo family abode, where famous 13th-century explorer Marco was born *(see p52)*. Other early Gothic buildings remain, their timber overhangs set off by bright red geraniums. Along with the adjoining bridge, the square was named in honour of the explorer whose marvellous stories about the Orient in his book *Il Milione* continue to inspire generations of travellers. ◈ Map Q2

Santa Maria dei Miracoli

A "jewellery box" of marble slabs and exquisite *bas-reliefs*, this Renaissance church was named after a miracle-working icon from 1409, said to have resuscitated a drowned man and now enshrined in the main altar *(see p38)*. ◈ Campo dei Miracoli, Cannaregio • Map Q2 • 041 275 04 62 • Open 10am–5pm Mon–Sat, 1–5pm Sun • Admission charge

Campo dei Mori

In this odd funnel-shaped square your attention is drawn to three statues of Arabian-style "Moors" – but neither North African nor Muslim, they hailed from Morea in Greece. Rioba, Sandi and Afani Mastelli were medieval traders who made

95

Medicinal potions, Farmacia Ponci

their home in the family palace around the corner. Next to the bridge over Rio della Sensa is a doorway marked No. 3399, once the residence of the renowned 16th-century artist Tintoretto *(see p44).* ◈ *Map D1*

Farmacia Ponci
The "Casa degli Speziali", the oldest pharmacy in Venice, carries on its business in modern premises alongside its restored 16th-century rooms. Displayed on original briarwood shelving adorned with Baroque statues in Arolla pinewood, are rows of 17th-century porcelain jars for medicinal ingredients; for safety reasons poisons were kept in a rear room. Pharmacies were strictly regulated and totalled 518 in 1564, the year their guild was formed. ◈ *Strada Nova, Cannaregio 2233A • Map D2*

Fondamente della Misericordia and degli Ormesini
Parallel to the Strada Nova but worlds away from the tourist bustle, these adjoining quaysides have a real neighbourhood feel. There's a good sprinkling of *osterie* (wine bars) alongside Mexican and Middle Eastern restaurants, a continuation of former trade links: the word *"ormesini"* derives from a rich fabric traded through Hormuz, now in Iran, and imitated in Florence and Venice. Ormesini leads into Misericordia and to the towering red-brick Scuola Grande building. Currently closed for restructuring, it served as the city's basketball team headquarters for many years. ◈ *Map C2*

Palazzo Labia façade

Palazzo Labia
The fames and fortunes of this 17th-century palace overlooking the Canal di Cannaregio could fill a book. Abandoned when its wealthy merchant owners fled to Vienna at the fall of the Republic, it acted as a silk factory, saw-mill and primary school, but the worst damage was inflicted in 1945 when a boat loaded with munitions blew up right in front of it. Luckily the wonderful ballroom frescoed by Tiepolo has been restored. The palace now belongs to RAI, the Italian state broadcasting service. ◈ *Campo S Geremia, Cannaregio • Map C2 • Ballroom: open 3–4pm Wed–Fri by appointment only (041 781 111)*

Chiesa di San Giobbe

Set in a peaceful square, this church is a bit of a hotchpotch after undergoing numerous architectural modifications before it was suppressed under Napoleon. An oratory and a paupers' hospital, it was founded in the 14th-century, with funding from Doge Cristoforo Moro and decorations by Pietro Lombardo. Superb altarpieces by Giovanni Bellini and Vittorio Carpaccio now hang in the Accademia Galleries *(see pp24–5)*, but still here are a 1445 triptych by Vivarini in the sacristy and a lovely *Nativity* (1540) by Girolamo Savoldo.

⊗ *Campo S Giobbe, Cannaregio • Map B2 • Open 10am–noon, 3:30–6pm daily • Free*

Fondamente Nuove

This lagoon-side pavement, opposite the cemetery island of San Michele *(see p110)*, is an important jumping-off point for ferries to the northern islands and sports one of the city's rare petrol stations. The ample quaysides were not constructed and paved until the mid-1500s; until then the waterfront reached back to Titian's garden (No. 5113, Calle Larga dei Botteri) allowing him unobstructed views of the Alps on a clear day, which delighted this native of Cadore.

⊗ *Map E2*

The Jews in Venice

Banned by Republic law from practising manual trades, many Jews were skilled doctors or money-lenders. Most were refugees from other parts of Europe, and they are credited with introducing rice-based dishes to Venetian cuisine. As remembered by a memorial in the Ghetto, few returned from the Nazi camps of World War II.

Exploring Cannaregio

Morning

Begin the day with the Galleria Franchetti in the lovely **Ca d'Oro** *(see p95)*, but leave plenty of time for the balconies which overlook the Grand Canal and the mosaics in the courtyard. Afterwards follow Strada Nova in the direction of the railway station to the Bottega del Caffè *(Calle del Pistor, Cannaregio 1903 • 041 714 232 • Closed Sat pm & Sun)* for the best coffee in Cannaregio. Only minutes away is the fascinating **Jewish Ghetto** *(see p95)*, where you can take a guided tour to the many remaining synagogues in the area.

For a revitalising break, lunch at Hostaria alla Fontana is recommended *(Fondamenta di Cannaregio, Cannaregio 1102 • 041 715 077 • Closed Sun)*.

Afternoon

Wander up the canal towards **Ponte dei Tre Archi** *(see p46)* and the **Chiesa di San Giobbe**. Return back over the bridge and make your way to Fondamenta della Sacca, which affords good views of the Dolomites in clear conditions. Many ways lead east from here, but try and take in the church of **Madonna dell'Orto** *(see p39)* for the Tintoretto paintings, then **Campo dei Mori** *(see p95)*.

Back on Strada Nova, an energetic young team awaits at La Cantina with a pre-dinner glass of wine from their north Italian range *(Strada Nova, Cannaregio 3689 • 041 522 82 58 • Closed Sun)*.

Left **Tàkalá** Right **Le Ragazze di Cima**

TOP 10 Specialist Shops

1 Tàkalá
Close to Campo SS Apostoli, a gift shop of fascinating holograms, Murano glass delights and chunky jewellery. ◈ *Strada Nova, Cannaregio 4391/C • Map D2*

2 The Body Shop
Famed for its strong stance against animal testing and its familiar extensive range of irresistible quality bodycare products. ◈ *Strada Nuova, Cannaregio 3844 • Map D2*

3 San Leonardo Market
In the morning and late afternoon this area functions as a lively open-air produce market. In autumn the air is thick with the aroma of roasting chestnuts. ◈ *Rio Terrà San Leonardo • Map C2 • Mon–Sat*

4 Lili e Paolo Darin
Original handmade glass beads in brilliant hues and myriad shapes, window hangings and Christmas decorations. ◈ *Salizzada S Geremia, Cannaregio 317 • Map C2*

5 TSL Tessile San Leonardo
Few passers-by manage not to be tempted by the great value velvety bathrobes, cut-price bed linen and fluffy towels here. ◈ *Rio Terrà S Leonardo, Cannaregio 1318, • Map C2*

6 Le Ragazze di Cima
Need a bridal trousseau or just a swimming costume? Lingerie for all occasions in silk and other fabrics can be found here. ◈ *Strada Nova, Cannaregio 3683/84 • Map D2*

7 Salmoiraghi & Vigano
Italian spectacles are stylish and good value, and this well-reputed optometrist can make up prescription glasses the same day. ◈ *Strada Nova, Cannaregio 3928-3930 • Map D2*

8 Barbara Boutique
Eye-catching window displays of sophisticated ladies' fashion. Good range of stock changing from season to season. ◈ *Fondamenta Ormesini, Cannaregio 2686 • Map C2*

9 Libreria Giunti
Large bookshop minutes from the railway station open until midnight seven days a week. A good stock of literature in English. ◈ *Campo S Geremia, Cannaregio 282 • Map C2*

10 Principe
Branches of this women's fashion store can be found all over Venice. The latest in trendy designs at value prices. ◈ *Rio Terrà S Leonardo, Cannaregio 1332 • Map C2*

For more on shopping in Venice **See p138**

Left **Ristorante Al Fontego dei Pescaori** Right **Osteria al Bacco**

Places to Eat

1 Ristorante Al Fontego dei Pescaori

Classy seafood restaurant with a lovely courtyard for summer dining, noted for its seasonal specialities. ✪ Sottoportego del Tagiapiera, Cannaregio 3711 • Map D2 • 041 520 0538 • Closed Tue • No disabled access • €€–€€€

2 Il Gelatone

Try ice cream maestro Michele's bacio (kiss) of hazelnut and chocolate. ✪ Rio Terrà Maddalena, Cannaregio 2063 • Map D2 • 041 720 631 • €

3 Brek

A self-service restaurant open from breakfast to dinner, everything prepared as you wait. ✪ Lista di Spagna, Cannaregio 124 • Map B2 • 041 244 0158 • €

4 Trattoria Pontini da Giada e Roberta

The set menu here is excellent value, or try the innovative salads and apple strudel. ✪ Ponte delle Guglie, Cannaregio 1268 • Map C2 • 041 714 123 • Closed Sun and winter D • €

5 Bar Matteo

An unbeatable range of sandwiches. Eat in or take away. ✪ Ponte delle Guglie, Cannaregio 321–326 • Map C2 • Closed Sun • €

6 Sahara

Delicious Arab fare at low prices, such as Magluba, a rice dish with almonds, pine nuts, beef and aubergine (eggplant). ✪ Fondamenta della Misericordia, Cannaregio 2519 • Map D2 • 041 721 077 • €

7 Antica Mola

Friendly family trattoria with a garden and canalside dining. ✪ Fondamenta degli Ormesini, Cannaregio 2800 • Map C2 • 041 717 492 • Closed Aug • €€

8 Pizza e poi

Oven-fresh take-away pizza, smothered with both traditional and innovative toppings. ✪ Strada Nova, Cannaregio 2222 • Map D2 • 041 522 8671 • €

9 Osteria Anice Stellato

Book well ahead for this popular place serving fish, meat and a wonderful zabaglione dessert. ✪ Fondamenta della Sensa, Cannaregio 3272 • Map C1 • 041 720 744 • Closed Mon, Tue & 2 weeks Aug • €€€

10 Osteria al Bacco

Fish-only restaurant with a garden. Try the spicy spaghetti alla busara, with prawns, tomato and chilli. ✪ Fondamenta delle Cappuccine, Cannaregio 3054 • Map C1 • 041 717 493 • Closed Mon, 2 weeks Jan and Aug • €€

Left **Riva degli Schiavoni** Right **San Pietro di Castello**

Castello

NAMED AFTER A CASTLE *possibly built here in Roman times, Castello is the "fishtail" of Venice. The western half of the district is crammed with* historic highlights such as the churches of SS Giovanni e Paolo and San Zaccaria. However, half of Castello is taken up with shipbuilding, focusing on the historic Arsenale. The tree-lined Giardini is the venue for the Biennale (see p102).

Sights

1. Riva degli Schiavoni
2. Hotel Danieli
3. Santa Maria della Pietà
4. Arsenale
5. San Pietro di Castello
6. Campo Santi Giovanni e Paolo
7. Campo Santa Maria Formosa
8. Via Garibaldi and Giardini
9. Chiesa di San Francesco della Vigna
10. Ospedaletto

Statue, Santa Maria Formosa

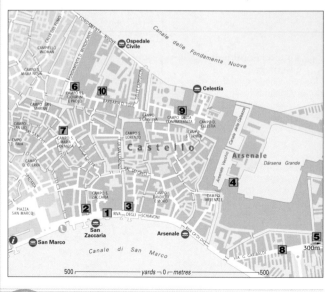

1 Riva degli Schiavoni

Thronging with tour groups and packed with souvenir stalls, this quayside affords a lovely promenade past majestic palaces (now mostly hotels) and a much photographed 1887 monument to the first king of Italy, Vittorio Emanuele. It is linked to Piazza San Marco by the elegant Istrian stone bridge Ponte della Paglia, named after the straw *(paglia)* once unloaded from barges here. This is also the best place for taking pictures of the Bridge of Sighs. At the eastern end is the Ca' di Dio ("house of God"), a 13th-century hospice for pilgrims en route to the Holy Land.
⊗ *Map F4*

2 Hotel Danieli

An enchanting 15th-century palace with a pink Gothic façade set on the magnificent waterfront near Piazza San Marco. After a string of aristocratic proprietors, it was taken over in 1822 by Joseph da Niel, who turned it into a hotel with an illustrious guest list, including Dickens, Wagner and Ruskin. In the 1940s an annexe was added amid great controversy – since 1102 no dwelling over one floor had been allowed on the site. The redeeming feature of the new wing is the roof restaurant *(see p144).*

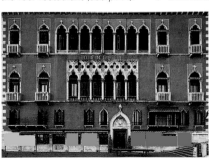

Gothic arches, Hotel Danieli

3 Santa Maria della Pietà

Inextricably linked with the composer and musician Antonio Vivaldi, this Classical-fronted church belonged to the adjoining home for foundlings where he taught. Come to an evening concert to appreciate Tiepolo's uplifting ceiling fresco exalting music and the young orphan choristers, identifiable by their sprigs of pomegranate blossom. The interior has choir stalls to accommodate both the singers and nobility who were not expected to mingle with the commoners. ⊗ *Riva degli Schiavoni, Castello 3700 • Map F4*

4 Arsenale

Aptly named after the Arab word *darsina'a* (which means "house of industry"), Venice's formidable Arsenale shipyards at their height once employed an army of 16,000 to produce the fleets that sailed the Mediterranean, spreading and protecting the influence of the Republic through trade deals and naval superiority. Justifiably proud of its innovative assembly-line system, the Arsenale could construct a galley in a matter of hours, notably in 1574 while the French king Henry III was enjoying a banquet. Ringed by walls and towers bearing the winged lion, some of its ancient docks and workshops are now being adapted as exhibition and performance venues *(see p54).* The row of stone lions which are guarding the entrance hail from various Greek islands looted by Venetian commanders. ⊗ *Castello • Map G3*

5 San Pietro di Castello

A sleepy island of grassy squares and boatyards, it is hard to imagine that Venice's religious headquarters were centred here right up until 1807, when the Basilica San Marco became the city's cathedral. Linked to the rest of Castello by two broad bridges, San Pietro attracts artists for its evocative forlorn air and fun-lovers for the animated late-June neighbourhood fair. Art lovers also come for the church with work by Veronese and Coducci, flanked by the patriarchal palace-cum-army barracks.
Ⓢ *Chiesa di San Pietro di Castello • Map H4 • Open 10am–5pm Mon–Sat, 1–5pm Sun • Admission charge*

6 Campo Santi Giovanni e Paolo

Dominated by the brick façade of the Gothic church SS Giovanni e Paolo, this breezy square welcomes visitors with a flotilla of outdoor cafés. Worthy of contemplation is one of the world's most magnificent equestrian statues, a stylized 15th-century portrait of the great *condottiere* Bartolomeo Colleoni. He left a legacy to the city on the condition that his statue be erected in front of San Marco, craftily "interpreted" by the governors as the Scuola Grande di San Marco close at hand. Gracefully

The Venice Biennale

The Giardini and its beautiful tree-lined avenues were inaugurated as an international exhibition area in 1895 under the entrepreneur Count Volpi di Misurata. Every two years more than 50 countries send artists to represent them, each with their own pavilion custom-designed by leading architects such as Alvar Aalto, Carlo Scarpa and James Stirling.

Tree-lined avenue in the Giardini

decorated with arches and *trompe l'oeil* panels by the Lombard masters, the former confraternity serves as the public hospital.
Ⓢ *Map E3*

7 Campo Santa Maria Formosa

A lovely rounded church on this sun-blessed square appears to spread in all directions, the result of a 7th-century bishop's vision of the "shapely" *(formosa)* Virgin Mary's request it be built where "a white cloud came to rest". Artworks are by Vivarini and Palma il Vecchio. The square is a good place for a picnic or a game of football, in lieu of the bullfights and re-enactments of Venice's conquests held here in olden days. Ⓢ *Chiesa di Santa Maria Formosa • Map E3 • Open 10am–5pm Mon–Sat, 1–5pm Sun • Admission charge*

8 Via Garibaldi and Giardini

A pleasant avenue now lined with cafés and a market, Via Garibaldi was triumphantly named when the eponymous general marched into Venice in 1866 as part of his round-Italy campaign for Unification. Take a stroll to the Giardini (public gardens). To make way for the park in 1807, architect Selva *(see p45)* demolished four churches and convents and a sailors' hospice.
Ⓢ *Map H5*

9 Chiesa di San Francesco della Vigna

In the back alleys of Castello, this Franciscan church sports a combination of architectural styles courtesy of both Sansovino and Palladio *(see p45)*, who designed the façade. The colonnaded cloister can be seen while you're appreciating Giovanni Bellini's *Madonna and Child* (1507). Playgrounds have replaced the 13th-century vineyards *(vigna)*.
§ *Campo S Francesco della Vigna, Castello 6691 • Map F3 • 041 520 61 02 • Open 8am–12:30pm, 3–7pm daily • Free*

10 Ospedaletto

For John Ruskin the sculptures on the façade of this almshouse church represented "masses of diseased figures and swollen fruit". Judge Longhena's controversial work was added in 1674. Pass through the less provocative interior of the church to the Sala della Musica. Female wards of the orphanage once gave concerts in this pretty room decorated with 18th-century frescoes.
§ *Barbarie delle Tole, Castello 6691 • Map F3 • Open 3:30–6:30pm Thu–Sat (Nov–Mar: 3–6pm) • Admission charge*

Longhena sculptures, Ospedaletto

A Day in Castello

Morning

After a visit to the Gothic church on **Campo Santi Giovanni e Paolo**, wander through the city's hospital. Although it is now ultra-modern inside, you can still appreciate the wonderful Renaissance façade, and a series of ancient courtyards and confraternity buildings. Continue the historic theme with a coffee and cake at old-style Rosa Salva *(Campo SS Giovanni e Paolo, Castello 6779 • 041 522 79 49).*

Take a stroll, via **Campo Santa Maria Formosa**, to Campo San Zaccaria and the church with its Bellini painting and **Scuola di San Giorgio degli Schiavoni** *(see p40)* for its Carpaccio works. For lunch, **Via Garibaldi** is a good bet, at one of the cafés or at Sottoprova *(041 520 64 93 • Closed Mon).*

Afternoon

Head east along Via Garibaldi and detour briefly into the shady avenue for the statue of Giuseppe Garibaldi and his followers. After a visit to the island of **San Pietro di Castello**, make your way back via the lagoon and the **Giardini**. A poignant sculpture to the female partisans of World War II can be seen at water level.

Heading in the direction of San Marco, just past the mouth of Via Garibaldi, on the embankment is Angiò Bar, the perfect spot for a Venetian sunset together with a glass of wine, not to mention all manner of delicious snacks *(Riva di S Biasio, Castello 2142 • 041 277 85 55 • Closed Tue).*

Left **Pastificio Le Spighe** Right **Chips and Colours**

Specialist Shops

1 Le Ceramiche
In a tiny atelier close to the Arsenale *(see p54)*, Alessandro Merlin creates original platters, cups and tiles, with black and white designs based on lagoon fish or human figures. ✆ *Calle del Pestrin, Castello 3876 • Map F4*

2 Pastificio Le Spighe
A normal grocery store at first sight, this hive of industry produces a marvellous range of homemade pasta and stocks gourmet olive oils and olive paste. ✆ *Via Garibaldi, Castello 1341 • Map G4*

3 Chips & Colours
Original printed Venice T-shirts and cloth bags are on sale in an old bakery re-used as an internet point and art gallery. ✆ *Via Garibaldi, Castello 1592 • Map G4*

4 Il Papiro
Tempting gifts in the shape of marbled paper-covered boxes, greeting cards and writing paper with artistic letterheads. ✆ *Calle delle Bande, Castello 5275 • Map E4*

5 Anticlea Antiquariato
Inviting boudoir filled with an amazing collection of glass beads and striking hat pins. Necklaces and earrings can be made up on the spot. ✆ *Calle S Provolo, Castello 4719/A • Map F4*

6 Mistero Atelier
Glorious Oriental emporium with a range of dazzling Thai and Indian silks made up to Italian designs for suits, scarves and ties. ✆ *Ruga Giuffa, Castello 4925 • Map F3*

7 Crovato
Contemporary light fittings in bold Italian designs and a great selection of coloured candles. ✆ *Ruga Giuffa, Castello 4920 • Map F3*

8 Corte delle Fate
Ultra-modern footwear and zany accessories in the shape of bags, jewellery and garments for the young. ✆ *Salizzada S Lio, Castello 5690 • Map E3*

9 Lanterna Magica
A toy and gadget shop where you can browse among star-studded umbrellas and "magic lantern" lamps with a procession of shadow figures. ✆ *Calle delle Bande, Castello 5379 • Map E3*

10 Giovanna Zanella
A must for all serious shoppers – zany handmade shoes and hats in a fabulous range of incredible designs. ✆ *Calle Carminati, Castello 5641 • Map Q3*

Price Categories

For a three-course meal for one with half a bottle of wine (or equivalent meal), taxes and extra charges

€	under €30
€€	€30–€40
€€€	€40–€50
€€€€	€50–€60
€€€€€	over €60

Left **Trattoria Giorgione** Right **Alla Rivetta**

Places to Eat

Taverna Olandese Volante
1 Lively bar serving draught beer and where the rolls are named after pirates and the salads after ships – try the "Galeone" with prawn and hard-boiled egg. ⊛ Campo S Lio, Castello 5658 • Map E3 • 041 528 9349 • Closed Sun L • €

Antica Pasticceria Venexiana
2 Wonderful savoury pastries and mini pizzas, for stand-up consumption at the bar or take-away. ⊛ Calle del Caffettier, Castello 6645 • Map F3 • 041 522 4483 • Closed Mon • €

Boutique del Gelato
3 There's inevitably a queue outside this popular *gelateria*. Try the tangy *limone* (lemon) or *fragola* (strawberry) ice cream or creamy *gianduiotto* (hazelnut-chocolate). ⊛ Salizzada S Lio, Castello 5727 • Map E3 • 041 522 3283 • Closed Dec–Jan • €

Osteria da Dante (Alle Alpi)
4 Low-ceilinged wine bar whose tables seem permanently occupied by card-playing men. Traditional counter fare such as *bovoleti* and *garusoli* (types of snails) and grilled sardines. ⊛ Corte Nova, Castello 277 • Map F4 • 041 528 5163 • Closed Sun • €

Trattoria Giorgione
5 After serving his fish specialities, owner Lucio entertains guests with Venetian folk songs. ⊛ Via Garibaldi, Castello 1533 • Map G4 • 041 522 8727 • Closed Wed • €€

Alla Rivetta
6 Friendly eatery with a wonderful seafood window display. ⊛ Ponte S Provolo, Castello 4625 • Map E4 • 041 528 7302 • Closed Mon • €€

Alla Mascareta
7 An upmarket bar for wine lovers, also serves meals. ⊛ Calle Lunga S Maria Formosa, Castello 5183 • Map E3 • 041 523 0744 • Closed lunch, Sun, 4 weeks Dec–Jan • €

Alle Testiere
8 Tiny, cosy restaurant with an unusual selection of fish, cheese and wines. ⊛ Calle del Mondo Novo, Castello, 5801 • Map F3 • 041 522 7220 • Closed Sun, Mon & Aug • €€€€

Hostaria ae Do Porte
9 Wood-lined tavern, noted for its grilled fish. Lunch only. ⊛ Corte delle Due Porte, Castello 6492 • Map F3 • 041 520 8842 • Closed Sun • €

Al Covo
10 Sophisticated candlelit fish dining and Italian wine list. ⊛ Campiello de la Pescaria, Castello 3968 • Map F4 • 041 522 3812 • Closed Wed–Thu, 4 weeks Dec–Jan, 1 week Aug • €€€€€

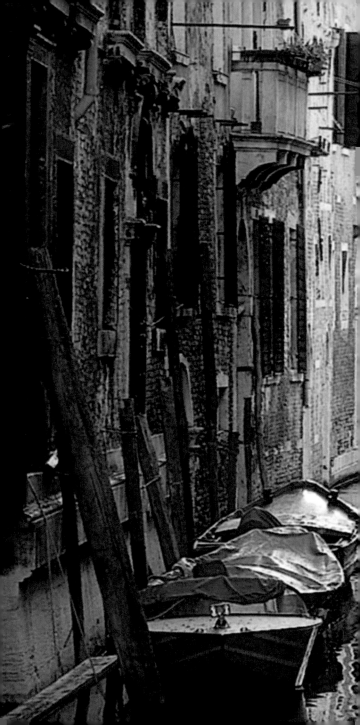

Left **San Michele** Right **Certosa**

The Northern Lagoon

THE NORTHERN LAGOON IS DOTTED WITH *mud flats and abandoned islands where rambling monasteries lie crumbling in the sun, backed by sweeping views of snow-capped mountains. Refugees from the mainland, fleeing the Huns, first settled on Torcello, which grew with the additional influx of influential religious orders. Today, however, only a handful of islands are still inhabited – glassmaking Murano is the most important, while Burano, Mazzorbo and Sant' Erasmo have skeletal populations of fishermen and market gardeners. Salt pans, such as Le Saline, were a source of employment until as late as 1913.*

Sights

1 Torcello
2 Burano
3 Murano
4 Mazzorbo
5 San Francesco del Deserto
6 San Michele
7 Sant'Erasmo
8 Lazzaretto Nuovo
9 Certosa
10 Punta Sabbioni

Murano

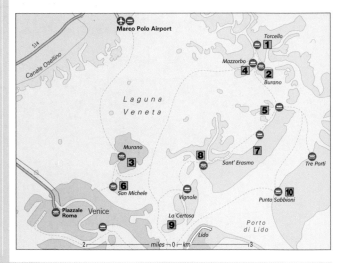

Preceding pages **Backwater canal, Venice**

1 Torcello

See pp30–31.

2 Burano

A haven for artists, brightly painted houses, fish and lace-making are the pride of Burano. The islanders cherish an old legend about a faithful sailor who resisted the Sirens' call and was rewarded with a magnificent veil of magical foam for his bride, later worked into lace, a trade that brought worldwide fame and fortune to the isolated fisherfolk. These days, although old women still strain their eyes with patient stitches, many articles are in fact imported from abroad. The island's dramatically leaning bell tower is visible from afar. ⊗ *Ferry No. LN from Fondamente Nuove or S Zaccaria • Map H1*

3 Murano

Long synonymous with glassmaking, Murano developed blowing and fusion techniques to extraordinary heights in the 1500s, and so closely guarded were the trade secrets that skilled crafts-men could migrate only under pain of death. Though Venice's glass monopoly lasted only until the 17th century, its fame lives on. A visit to the Glass Museum with its 4,000 exhibits is a must *(see p40)*. Don't be put off by the reps who invite tourists to see a furnace and showroom; it's a unique opportunity to watch the glassblowers at work and is free of charge. However, if you accept a free boat trip from San Marco to a glass factory, you're expect-ed to make your own way back by *vaporetto* if you don't buy any-thing. Glassmaking aside, Murano is a lovely place to wander around, with canals, alleyways and friendly islanders. ⊗ *Vaporetto lines 41 & 42 from Fondamente Nuove, DM from P Roma or seasonal lines • Map G2*

Torcello basilica

4 Mazzorbo

This pretty island of cats exudes a tranquil air as locals tend their vineyards or artichoke fields. Wicker cages for fattening up *moleche* (soft-shelled crabs) hang on racks over the water and the produce can be sampled in the low-key *trattorias*. Amid the scattering of houses are bold modern council blocks painted in pastel hues. Mazzorbo has its own boat stop but is also joined to Burano by a timber footbridge. ⊗ *Ferry No. LN from Fondamente Nuove or S Zaccaria • Map H1*

5 San Francesco del Deserto

A short distance from Burano, this attractive island of cypress trees is home to a Franciscan monastery. According to legend it was founded by St Francis in person, on his way back from preaching missions in Egypt and Palestine in 1220. In May, clad in their brown habits and sandals, the monks attend the Vogalonga in their heavy-duty boat, to the delight of the Venetians *(see p62)*. ⊗ *Taxi launch from Burano's landing stage • Map H1 • Monastery: open 9–11am, 3–5pm Tue–Sun • Donation*

Lagoon Flora and Fauna

The lagoon abounds in gilt-head bream, sea bass, clams, cuttlefish and crabs, which are all prey for wetland waterfowl such as swans, egrets, cormorants and the rare black-winged stilts. Sea lavender blooms on land masses, rock samphire clings to crumbling masonry, while glasswort thrives in the salt-ridden marshes.

San Michele

San Michele became the city cemetery in 1826, in the wake of a hygienic Napoleonic decree that the dead should be buried far from the dwellings of the living. Entry to the cemetery is via a lovely Gothic portal surmounted by St Michael at odds with a dragon, and through the monk's colonnaded cloister. But don't neglect to visit the pretty marble-façaded church next door, designed by Mauro Coducci in 1469 (see p45). On All Souls' Day (2 November), the place is crowded with relatives paying a visit to their dear departed. However unless you're a famous resident like Ezra Pound, Stravinsky or Diaghilev, your bones are dug up after 10 years and placed in an urn to make room for someone else. ॐ Ferry Nos. 41 & 42 from Fondamente Nuove • Map G2 • Cemetery: open 7:30am–6pm daily (closes 4pm Oct–Mar)

Sant'Erasmo

Unflattering jokes circulate about the inhabitants of Sant' Erasmo, with reference to in-breeding. However, no one would dare to question their ability to produce delicious asparagus and artichokes which

prosper on the sandy soil and are a mainstay of Rialto Market (see p28). Just over 4 km (2.5 miles) long and 1 km (0.5 miles) at the broadest point, Sant' Erasmo offers a tranquil countryside, praised enthusiastically by the Romans who built sumptuous villas here. A couple of rickety old motor cars occasionally bump along the lanes, but bicycles and boats are still the main form of transport. ॐ Ferry No. 13 from Fondamente Nuove • Map H2

Lazzaretto Nuovo

Across the water from Sant' Erasmo, up until the 1700s this island served as a quarantine station for merchant ships entering the lagoon and suspected of carrying the plague. Together with neighbouring Sant' Erasmo it housed up to 10,000 people during the 1576 pestilence, while cargoes were fumigated with rosemary and juniper in temporary shelters. Later converted into a military stronghold, it now swarms with archaeology enthusiasts intent on unearthing its secrets and students attending summer camps. ॐ Ferry No. 13 from Fondamente Nuove • Map H2 • Tours Apr–Oct: 9:45am & 4pm Sat–Sun

Sant' Erasmo

Punta Sabbioni

Certosa
9 Inhabited by religious communities for more than 600 years, the "charterhouse" island went the way of many of its neighbours under occupation by French, Austrian and Italian forces, though currently as the property of the City Council, is slowly being cleaned up as a public park. Though there is no public boat service, it can be seen from *vaporetto* lines as they circle eastern Castello. Also clearly visible from the Lido-Punta Sabbioni ferry are the impressive fortified ramparts of Sanmicheli's 16th-century Forte di Sant'Andrea, which faced any hostile vessels that dared to enter the lagoon unbidden. ◈ *Map H2*

Punta Sabbioni
10 This locality clings to the promontory extending westward from the mainland – a continuous string of beach resorts equipped with spacious camp sites. Alongside sleepy backwaters and canals is Punta Sabbioni ("big sandy point") a busy bus-ferry terminal that bustles with summer holiday-makers. It came into being as sand accumulated behind the 1,100-m (3,600-ft) breakwater erected to protect the port mouth and littoral, and offers lovely seaside strolls. ◈ *Ferry No LN from Lido or Burano*

Sailing the Lagoon

Morning

🕐 To save money, buy a *laguna nord* day ticket *(see p135)* then take a vaporetto to **Murano** *(see p109)* to watch a glassmaking demonstration at a furnace or one of the workshops. Don't miss Murano's very own Grand Canal, before returning via Fondamenta Manin with its medieval porticoes for the turn-off towards the Faro (light-house) landing stage. Bar al Faro is a perfect place for coffee. *(Fondamenta Piave 20, Murano • 041 739 724 • Closed Sun).*

Take a ferry to **Burano** *(see p109)*. Either picnic on the famous Burano biscuits or lunch at Da Romano. A popular meeting place for artists *(Piazza Galuppi 221, Burano • 041 730 030 • Closed Tue & Sun dinner, mid-Dec–early Feb)*.

Afternoon

Pop over to **Torcello** *(see pp30–31)* by ferry for the awe-inspiring Byzantine mosaics in the basilica. Climb the bell tower for unbeatable views of the lagoon, and the mountains if visibility is favourable.

Return to the water on a ferry via Burano south past low-lying islands and tidal flats. A stretch parallel to the sandy littoral separating the lagoon from the Adriatic Sea takes you to **Punta Sabbioni**, where a stopover is feasible for a drink on the jetty.

End the day sailing across the broad lagoon mouth, via the **Lido** *(see p115)*, back to **Piazza San Marco** *(see pp16–19)*.

Left **Barovier & Toso showroom** Centre and right **Mazzega**

Specialist Shops

Cesare Sent
This talented artist from a long line of glassmakers, transforms the ancient art of murrhine glassware into striking modern objects. Fondamenta Vetrai 8b, Murano • Map G2

ArtStudio
Watch glass artist Davide Penso at work producing marvellous African-inspired glass beads. Fondamenta Rivalonga 48, Murano • Map G2

Manin 56
Striking etched bowls and slender wine glasses from Salviati flank international designer items in this wonderful collection. Fondamenta Manin 56, Murano • Map G2

Murano Collezioni
A stunning new showroom containing contemporary pieces by Carlo Moretti and Venini, alongside classic light fittings by Barovier & Toso. Fondamenta Manin 1/CD, Murano • Map G2

Barovier & Toso
The world's oldest family of glassmakers, the Baroviers are able to trace their ancestry back to the 13th century. They still produce stunning contemporary pieces. Fondamenta Vetrai 28, Murano • Map G2

Mazzega
Vast showrooms display traditional and semi-modern glass designs with an emphasis on chandeliers and vases. Fondamenta da Mula 147, Murano • Map G2

CAM
The first shop you see as you disembark at Murano, this internationally known firm specializes in distinctive modern pieces. Piazzale Colonna 1, Murano • Map G2

Pastificio e Panificio Giorgio Garbo
Sample Burano's trademark vanilla-flavoured shortbread, *bussolai*, freshly baked in traditional rounds or "S" shapes. Via S Mauro 336, Burano • Map H1

Gianna G
Here delicate lace handkerchiefs are sewn on a traditional cylindrical cushion. Via S Mauro 332, Burano • Map H1

Lidia Merletti d'Arte
While the front of the shop is an emporium of lace tablecloths, hand towels and mats, the rear is a gallery with a priceless 18th-century wedding gown, a lace fan owned by Louis XIV and lace altarpieces. Via Galuppi 215, Burano • Map H1

Lidia Merletti d'Arte

 For more on shopping in Venice See p138

Left **Antica Trattoria alla Maddalena** Right **Al Gatto Nero**

🔟 Places to Eat

1 Trattoria Busa alla Torre, Da Lele

Dine inside under timber rafters or outside in the square. Start with soft-shelled *moleche* (crab) or ravioli filled with fish, but leave room for the nougat pastries. Open for lunch only. ✪ *Campo S Stefano 3, Murano • Map G2 • 041 739 662 • Open for lunch only • No disabled access • €€*

2 Panificio Giovanni Marcato

Delicious slices of pizza with tomato and olives, and traditional *zaletti* biscuits or luscious *pincetto*, sponge cake with chocolate. ✪ *Fondamenta Rivalonga 16, Murano • Map G2 • 041 739 176 • €*

3 Osteria La Perla Ai Bisatei

Home-style cooking at reasonable prices. The *fritto misto* seafood is superb. Open for lunch only. ✪ *Campo S Bernardo 6, Murano • Map G2 • 041 739 528 • No credit cards • No disabled access • €*

4 Trattoria Valmarana

Stylish eating on a waterside terrace near the Glass Museum (*see p41*). Try *rombo al forno con patate e olive* (baked flounder with potatoes and olives). ✪ *Fondamenta Navagero 31, Murano • Map G2 • 041 739 313 • €€*

5 Trattoria Al Corallo

A popular, chaotic trattoria. Dine on fresh fish by the canal. Open for lunch only. ✪ *Fondamenta Vetrai 73, Murano • Map G2 • 041 739 636 • Closed Tue • €*

6 Trattoria ai Cacciatori

Cheaper and quieter than neighbouring Burano, here you can savour potato dumplings with crab and, in autumn, local game. ✪ *Mazzorbo 23 • Map H1 • 041 730 118 • Closed Mon and Dec–mid-Feb • €*

7 Antica Trattoria alla Maddalena

Renowned for its spring artichokes and roast duck, this laidback trattoria also serves a light, local white wine. Lunch and early dinner only. ✪ *Mazzorbo 7B • Map H1 • 041 730 151 • Closed Thu • €*

8 Al Gatto Nero

Wonderful al fresco fish restaurant, surrounded by Burano's colourful houses. ✪ *Fondamenta Giudecca 88, Burano • Map H1 • 041 730 120 • Closed Mon, 1st week Jul, 2 weeks Nov • No disabled access • €€€€*

9 Locanda Cipriani

Meals in this historic establishment are served on the terrace. The house speciality is *filetto di San Pietro Carlina* (baked John Dory with tomato and capers) ✪ *Piazza S Fosca 29, Torcello • Map H1 • 041 730 150 • Closed Tue, Jan • No disabled access • €€€€€*

10 Ca' Vignotto

Book in advance to eat at this rambling farmhouse turned trattoria. Dishes include dumplings with crab and artichokes or asparagus lasagne. ✪ *Via Forti 71, S Erasmo • Map H2 • 041 528 5329 • Closed Tue, evenings Nov–Apr, 1 week Jan • €*

 Note: *Unless otherwise stated, all restaurants accept credit cards and serve vegetarian meals*

Left **San Giorgio** Centre **San Lazzaro garden** Right **San Servolo artist at work**

The Southern Lagoon and Venice Lido

THE SOUTHERN LAGOON ENJOYS *protection from the Adriatic Sea with shifting sand spits long transformed into a permanent littoral, the residential Lido, with the ongoing help of nature and man. The latter's efforts date back to the 6th century, but the earth and wicker barriers have since been modified into sturdy seawalls and massive parallel breakwaters at the shipping entrances of San Nicolò, Alberoni and Chioggia. On the lagoon's southwestern edge are fish farms and wild shallows where hunters and fishermen still roam, well clear of the Valle Averto reserve run by the World Wildlife Fund for Nature (WWF). Closer to Venice itself is a cluster of sizeable islands such as majestic San Giorgio and populous Giudecca, then diminutive land masses such as a lazaret, where plague victims were once quarantined but which has now been re-adapted as a home for stray dogs, a sanatorium acquired for private development as an exclusive resort, and countless other evocative abandoned places.*

TOP 10 Sights

1. San Giorgio
2. Giudecca
3. Lido: San Nicolò
4. Lido: beach side
5. Lido: Malamocco
6. San Lazzaro degli Armeni
7. Santa Maria delle Grazie
8. San Servolo
9. San Pietro in Volta & Pellestrina
10. Chioggia

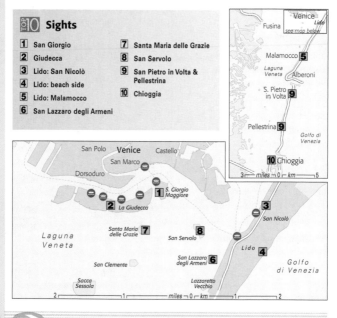

1 San Giorgio

The island of cypresses is separated from the main body of Venice by St Mark's Basin and retains a quiet meditative air, unconcerned with the bustle in the city. An ancient vineyard and salt pans were replaced by a landmark church by Andrea Palladio *(see p45)*, adjoining an elegant Benedictine monastery. It is now a scientific and cultural foundation and conference centre. At the rear is the open-air amphitheatre Teatro Verde, which is used for performances of contemporary dance and music *(see p62)*. ✆ *Fondazione Giorgio Cini (vaporetto No. 82) • Open 10am–5pm Sat & Sun guided visits (041 524 0119) • Admission charge*

2 Giudecca

An S-shaped slice of land facing the sun-blessed Zattere, this residential garden island was first known as "Spina longa" for its fishbone form. It was renamed either after an early Jewish community, or the *giudicati* (radical aristocrats) exiled here. Renaissance artist Michelangelo spent three peaceful years here in voluntary exile from 1529. Much later it became an important industrial zone with shipbuilding and the immense Molino Stucky flour mill *(see p54)*. Usually quiet and neighbourly, it comes to life with a vengeance for the mid-July Redentore festivities *(see p62)*. ✆ *Vaporetto Nos. 82, 41, 42*

3 Lido: San Nicolò

The northern end of the Lido littoral, a key point in the Republic's defence, used to be equipped with impressive naval fortifications and chains would be laid across the lagoon mouth as a deterrent to invaders. The historic Sensa celebration *(see p62)* is held offshore from the church of San Nicolò, founded in 1044 and a former Benedictine monastery, now a study centre. One visitable site is the 1386 Jewish cemetery. Alternatively, take a 35-minute mini-cruise on the car ferry between Tronchetto car park and San Nicolò. Its high decks give great views all over Venice. ✆ *Jewish Cemetery: Bus A from S Maria Elisabetta or car ferry from Tronchetto • 041 715 359 • Guided visits in English, booking essential • Admission charge*

4 Lido: beach side

Manicured sand raked daily and neat rows of multicoloured bathing cabins and beach umbrellas sum up the Lido from June to September, made famous in Thomas Mann's novel *Death in Venice (see p50)*. Venetians spend their summers socializing in style here. Things liven up considerably for the 10-day International Film Festival in September *(see p66)*, when the shady streets are filled with film buffs and critics on bicycles. ✆ *Ferry lines Nos. 1, LN, 51, 52, 61, 62*

Sunbathers, Lido beach resort

Heyday of the Lido

Evidence of the Lido's "golden age" as Europe's leading seaside resort at the turn of the 20th century can still be seen in the magnificent Art Deco villas. Exemplary survivors are the Hotel des Bains and the Excelsior, built in 1907 as the world's largest hotel, complete with mock minarets. Before that, the Lido was appreciated for its healthy air.

Lido: Malamocco

About midway along the Lido is the pretty, quiet village of Malamocco and it's now hard to imagine that it used to be the most important lagoon settlement soon after Roman times and the main port for Padua. A storm and giant waves washed away the entire town in 1106, later rebuilt in the vicinity on a smaller scale. It is appreciated for its 15th-century buildings, peaceful nature and rustic trattorias. ✆ *Bus No. 11 or lines B or V from S Maria Elisabetta*

San Lazzaro degli Armeni

Venice made a gift of this erstwhile leper colony to the Armenian monk, the Venerable Mechtar, forced out of the Peloponnese during one of his country's *diasporas*. Intent on fostering the Armenian culture and language, he founded a religious community here and set up a printing press which operated until 1994, publishing works in 36 languages. Multilingual monks instruct visitors in their history and lead guided tours through a small museum and an impressive library of more than 100,000 volumes and precious illuminated manuscripts. ✆ *Ferry line No. 20 from San Zaccaria • Open 3:20–5pm daily • Admission charge*

Santa Maria delle Grazie

Close to San Giorgio, this abandoned island used to be a hospice for pilgrims and was named after a miraculous image of the Virgin brought back from Constantinople and attributed to St Luke. Its colourful history features a series of religious orders and churches, devastating fires, allotments, luxuriant gardens and, until recently, the city's infectious diseases hospital. It is now private property with no public access.

San Servolo

In 1648, 200 nuns exiled from Candia, Crete, by the Turks were lodged on this island, but after their numbers dwindled in 1725 it was given over to a sanatorium for psychiatric cases, although exclusively those of "comfortable circumstances". The roomy buildings are now shared by an international university and a trade school for artisans from all over Europe interested in restoration of stone and stucco techniques. ✆ *Ferry No. 20 from San Zaccaria • Guided visits 11:30am, 2:45pm (book ahead 041 524 0119)*

Malamocco on the Lido

Traditional net-mending in Chioggia

9 San Pietro in Volta and Pellestrina

This narrow 11-km (6.5-mile) central strip of land, linked to the Lido and Chioggia by ferry, is dotted with picturesque sleepy fishing communities, once famous for lacemaking and now renowned for champion rowers and a shipyard. The Genoese wiped out the villages during the 14th century, an event almost repeated during the disastrous 1966 floods – powerful waves broke over the seawall, forcing full-scale evacuation. The massive defensive barriers with their 14-m (46-ft) broad base were first erected in the 1700s but have consequently needed large-scale reinforcement. *Bus No. 11 and ferry from the Lido or from Chioggia*

10 Chioggia

A lively fishing town, with elegant bridges over navigable canals. The friendly inhabitants have a reputation for lawlessness and bickering, and speak a distinctive dialect with a sing song inflection. Chioggia has a rich history, but its greatest moment came as the arena for the decisive battle in the 1378–9 war, when the Genoese came close to conquering Venice. In flat-bottomed boats the crafty locals enticed the enemy into the lagoon, thus gaining the upper hand. *Ferry from Pellestrina or bus from Piazzale Roma*

A Day on the Lagoon

Morning

From the Santa Maria Elisabetta ferry stop, either hire a bicycle or take buses B or V southwest along the lagoon edge for **Malamocco**. Wander through the peaceful village and over its bridge to the sea to take in the Adriatic and the impressive seawall. Then proceed with buses B or 11 through Alberoni and past the golf course for the vehicle ferry across the lagoon entrance. Get off at the second stop for **San Pietro in Volta**. Climb the high seawall for views of the sea, before turning lagoon-wards for the pastel-painted fishing settlement spread along the waterfront.

Have lunch at one of the trattorias *(see p119)* or a sandwich and glass of wine at one of the modest waterfront bars.

Afternoon

Further south the bus terminates at **Pellestrina**, a brightly painted fishing village flanked by an active shipyard. The passenger ferry to **Chioggia** is a beautiful half-hour cruise past mussel grounds punctuated with fisher huts perched on poles, via the Ca' Roman landing stage, which provides access to a beach. Chioggia is a lovely town to explore, with its traffic-free piazza lined with old palazzos and countless fish restaurants.

Indulge in a pre-dinner drink and snack at one of the laidback cafés in the elegant Corso del Popolo.

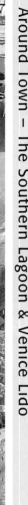

Left **Rizzo** Centre **Erbalido** Right **Arbor Boutique**

🔟 Shops and Markets

1 Rizzo
Unbeatable gourmet food from all over Italy – buffalo mozzarella, creamy Asiago cheese, cured Parma ham and gleaming olives. Pizza and *focaccia* can be found at the bread counter.
◈ *Gran Viale 18/20, Lido • Map H2*

2 General Market
Open-sided vans sell fresh produce, alongside designer-quality clothes, shoes and bags at approachable prices. Even if you don't buy anything, the lagoon setting looking over to the Venice skyline makes a trip worthwhile. ◈ *Via Falier, Lido • Map H2 • Tue am*

Confectionery at Rizzo

3 Erbalido
A traditional herbalist who can advise on natural remedies for minor ailments. ◈ *Via Negroponte 4/c, Lido • Map H2*

4 Arbor Boutique
The up-market range of mens- and womenswear attracts both foreign and Italian customers. ◈ *Santa Maria Elisabetta 10, Lido • Map H2*

5 Bruno Lazzari
This well-stocked bike shop rents out all normal steeds as well as 4-wheeler family models.
◈ *Viale Santa Maria Elisabetta 21/B, Lido • Map H2*

6 Oviesse-Billa
Department store with fashionable, moderately priced clothing for all ages, combined with a supermarket with a great selection of picnic products. ◈ *Gran Viale, Lido • Map H2*

7 Benetton
Small store but well-stocked with stylish clothes for the young.
◈ *Gran Viale 47b, Lido • Map H2*

8 El Penelo
Giorgio Boscolo is an expert on traditional fishermen's clay pipes and the only craftsman still to make them in terracotta and coloured glazes.
◈ *Palazzo Granaio Corso del Popolo, Chioggia • Map F1*

9 Carlo Bullo
Ignore the trinkets here and focus on the handcrafted models of *bragozzo* boats *(see p22)* painted in primary colours.
◈ *Corso del Popolo 1350, Chioggia • Map F1*

10 Panificio Sergio
These dry biscuits were traditionally made for seafarers. *Pevarini* are spicy rings with molasses and aniseed, while *Dolce del Doge* is spread with a chocolate-hazelnut mixture.
◈ *Stradale Ponte Caneva 626, Chioggia • Map F1*

Price Categories

For a three-course meal for one with half a bottle of wine (or equivalent meal), taxes and extra charges

€	under €30
€€	€30–€40
€€€	€40–€50
€€€€	€50–€60
€€€€€	over €60

Left **Harry's Dolci** Right **Los Murales**

🔟 Places to Eat

1 Altanella
Treat yourself to a candlelit dinner on the terrace. Fish dishes such as *frittura mista* (assorted fried seafood) are the speciality. ⊗ *Calle delle Erbe, Giudecca 268 • Map E6 • 041 522 7780 • Closed Mon–Tue, Jan & Aug • No credit cards • No vegetarian options • No disabled access • €€€*

2 Harry's Dolci
With views across the Giudecca Canal, this is the "sweet" branch of Harry's Bar *(see p21)* serving sorbets and pastries. ⊗ *S Eufemia, Giudecca 773 • Map C6 • 041 522 4844 • Closed Nov–Easter • €€€€€*

3 Los Murales
Lively Italian/Mexican eatery with outdoor seating, views over to San Marco and non-stop music. ⊗ *Fondamenta della Croce, Giudecca 68–71 • Map E6 • 041 523 0004 • Closed Wed (Mar–Oct), Sun (Nov–Feb) • No disabled access • €*

4 Trattoria Scarso
This good-value family eatery has a lovely garden hung with fishing nets where you can linger over grilled fish or a fresh salad. ⊗ *Piazzale Malamocco 5, Malamocco • Map H2 • 041 770 834 • Closed Mon D, Tue, 15 Jan–15 Feb • €€*

5 Agriturismo Le Garzette
Locals celebrate family anniversaries here with the crispy *frittura di pesce* (fried fish). ⊗ *Lungomare Alberoni 32, Malamocco • Map H2 • 041 731 078 • Open Mar–Nov: Fri D–Sun D • No credit cards • €€€*

6 Trattoria Da Nane
Memorable fish restaurant and terrace with panoramic views. Its speciality is a *pasticcio di pesce* (seafood lasagne). ⊗ *Via Laguna 282, S Pietro in Volta • 041 527 9110 • Closed Mon, mid-Nov–mid-Mar • No vegetarian options • No disabled access • €€€€*

7 Ristorante da Memo
A modest seafood restaurant with outdoor tables. Try the shrimps, eel or sole. ⊗ *Via Portosecco 157 (S Pietro in Volta) • 041 527 9125 • Closed Tue, mid-Nov–Mar • €€€€*

8 Ristorante La Sgura
An enchanting setting on a quiet canal, this fish restaurant also has a great selection of meat. Try the *zuppa di pesce* (fish soup). ⊗ *Fondamenta Marangoni 1295, Chioggia • Map F1 • 041 403 232 • Closed Mon, Jan • €€*

9 Pizzeria Vecio Foghero
In a quiet courtyard through a portico. The patriotic, and delicious, *Pizza al tricolore* is topped with mozzarella, rocket (arugula) and tomatoes. ⊗ *Calle Scopici 91/B, Chioggia • Map F1 • 041 404 679 • Closed Tue • €*

10 Ristorante al Buon Pesce
Roomy and friendly family-style fish restaurant with a delicious range of fresh grilled fish or fried seafood. ⊗ *Stradale Ponte Caneva 625, Chioggia • Map F1 • 041 400 861 • Closed Wed, Dec • No vegetarian options • €*

> **Note:** Unless otherwise stated, all restaurants accept credit cards and serve vegetarian meals

Left **Bo University, Padua** Right **Ponte Scaligero, Verona**

Padua, Vicenza and Verona

A WEALTH OF ART CITIES PUNCTUATES *the fertile Veneto plain that stretches in a broad wedge north from the Po River to the foothills of the Dolomites. There is ample evidence of the presence of Romans and Venetians alike in the shape of fascinating amphitheatres and elegant palaces in places such as Verona and Vicenza, both towns recently declared World Heritage Sites by UNESCO. Moreover, amid vineyards of grapes pressed for light sparkling Prosecco and aromatic Bardolino are charming, little visited villas with ornamental gardens. Each town has its distinctive character: business-like Padua, yet with a richly artistic and religious heart; Vicenza, contained and proper in its country setting and equally famous for its goldsmiths and the architecture of Andrea Palladio; then romantic Verona, lazing on the banks of the mighty Adige River as it flows south swollen with snow-melt from the Alps. Highlights in each locality are all feasible as day-trips from Venice by train.*

TOP 10 Sights

1. Cappella degli Scrovegni
2. Bo University
3. Basilica del Santo
4. Piazza dei Signori
5. Teatro Olimpico
6. Palazzo Leoni Montanari
7. Verona Arena
8. Casa di Giulietta
9. Piazza delle Erbe
10. Museo Civico di Storia Naturale

Teatro Olimpico, Vicenza

Preceding pages **Veneto countryside**

1 Cappella degli Scrovegni

The sky-blue vault studded with gold stars in this glorious Paduan chapel seems to hover over Giotto's vibrant frescoes narrating the lives of Mary and Jesus. The Florentine artist (1266–1337) was summoned by Enrico Scrovegni to work on the chapel in 1305–06, to atone for the sins of his late father, a moneylender. Especially noteworthy of the 38 distinct scenes is the *Last Judgment* on the entrance wall, with ranks of helmeted, haloed and shield-bearing angels. Book well in advance and be prepared to wait in the "decontamination" chamber before the 15-minute visit. ◎ *Piazza Eremitani, Padua • Bus Nos. 3, 8, 10, 12 • 049 201 00 20 • Open 9am– 7pm daily • Online booking: www.cappella degliscrovegni.it • Admission charge*

Cappella degli Scrovegni, Padua

2 Bo University

The original lectern where Galileo Galilei held his lessons between 1592 and 1610 can be seen on the guided tour of Padua's historic university, founded in 1222 and second only to Bologna as Italy's oldest. The institution boasts the world's first anatomy theatre (1594) where dissections had to be carried out in great secrecy as the church forbade such practices. Other illustrious scholars of the university have included astronomer Copernicus

(1473–1543), Gabriel Fallopius (1523–62), who discovered the function of the Fallopian tubes, and Elena Lucrezia Corner Piscopia, the world's first woman graduate *(see p52)*. ◎ *Via VIII Febbraio 2, Padua • Bus Nos. 3, 8, 12 • By guided tour only, telephone for times and booking 049 820 9741 • Admission charge*

3 Basilica del Santo

Popularly referred to as "il Santo", Padua's revered site of pilgrimage was built in the 13th century to safeguard the mortal remains of St Anthony, a Franciscan monk and miracle worker from Portugal. Worshippers visit his gleaming tomb, encircled by burning candles, but his tongue is guarded in an intricate reliquary in the Treasury, recently recovered after being stolen. In architectural terms the basilica blends Romanesque, Gothic, Islamic and Byzantine elements with elegant arched loggias, minarets and domes, and is a treasure trove of art works by Sansovino, Tiepolo and Titian *(see p44)*. ◎ *Piazza del Santo, Padua • Bus Nos. 8, 18 • Open 6:30am–7pm daily • Free*

Basilica del Santo, Padua

Romeo and Juliet

There is no doubt that the Capulet and Montague families existed, though they were probably more friendly than William Shakespeare made out in his tragic 1594–5 play. However the world's most famous star-crossed lovers may actually have come from Vicenza, home town of Luigi Da Porto, author of the original 1530 account.

Piazza dei Signori

In addition to the cafés in Vicenza's main square, come to admire the buildings by Palladio, whose 16th-century designs shaped both his home town and architecture worldwide (see p45). The basilica boasts twin levels of colonnaded arches, opposite his Loggia del Capitaniato. A statue of the architect stands at the western end of the basilica. 🛇 Basilica Palladiana: • Piazza dei Signori, Vicenza • Open during exhibitions • Admission charge

Teatro Olimpico

A castle courtyard draped with creepers was chosen for this Vicenza theatre, designed by Palladio and completed by his disciple Vincenzo Scamozzi. The performing area is based on a Roman model, while the stage scenery is a replica of the city of Thebes, built for the inaugural play, Sophocles' Oedipus Rex, in 1585. Scaled statues and varying stage levels create clever tricks of perspective. 🛇 Piazza Matteotti 11, Vicenza • Open 9am–5pm Tue–Sun (Jul–Aug: 9am–7pm) • Admission charge

Palazzo Leoni Montanari

On the entrance portal of this lavishly decorated Baroque palace are carvings of writhing serpents, and Hercules is shown in the act of slaying the Hydra on the loggia. The masterpieces include 120 awe-inspiring Russian icons and 14 fascinating paintings by Pietro Longhi depicting scenes from 18th-century Venetian life and hanging in the frescoed "Room of the Four Continents". 🛇 Contra' Santa Corona 25, Vicenza • Open 10am–6pm Tue–Sun • Admission charge

Verona Arena

This massive Roman amphi-theatre from the 1st century AD and measures almost 140 m (460 ft) in length. The arcades and 44-level tiered seating for 22,000 people, that once rang with the cries of gladiator fights, now echo with arias from operas during the popular summer festival. Verdi's Aïda marked the inauguration in 1913, and is repeated every year. 🛇 Piazza Brà, Verona • 045 800 32 04 • Open Jul–Aug: 8:30am–2:30pm daily (to 6:30pm if no performance); Sep–Jun 8:30am–6:30pm Tue–Sun • Partial wheelchair access • Admission charge

Casa di Giulietta

Tourists flock to "Juliet's House", the 13th-century pre-sumed abode of the Shakespearean hero-ine. Complete with a pretty balcony (added in 1928...) the roman-tically inclined can imagine her uttering that immortal cry: "Romeo, Romeo, wherefore art thou Romeo?" The courtyard walls are

Piazza dei Signori, Vicenza

Piazza delle Erbe, Verona

plastered with multilingual graffiti left by lovers from all over the world. ✪ *Via Cappello 23, Verona • Open 8:30am–7:30pm Tue–Sun, 1:30–7:30pm Mon • Admission charge*

9 Piazza delle Erbe

Originally Verona's Roman forum, this picturesque square is still a great place for discussing business over a coffee. Parasols shade souvenirs at the animated market, watched over by a winged lion atop a column, vestige of Venetian domination. The 84-m (275-ft) Torre Lamberti offers great city views. ✪ *Torre dei Lamberti, Cortile Mercato Vecchio, Verona • Open 8:30am–7:30pm Tue–Sun, 1:30–7:30pm Mon • Admission charge*

10 Museo Civico di Storia Naturale

Gigantic ferns, weird fish and an ancestor of the crocodile, all in fossilized form from the Eocene era, 50 million years ago are treasures hailing from Bolca in the Lessini foothills. They testify to the tropical shallows that spread across the area prior to the formation of the Alps. ✪ *Lungadige Porta Vittoria 9, Verona • Open 9am–7pm Mon–Thu, Sat; 2–7pm Sun & hols • Admission charge*

A Day Out in Verona

Morning

Where better to begin than the inspiring **arena**, where wild animals once made a meal of gladiators as entertainment? Afterwards, relax in the sun with a creamy coffee at Liston 12 Caffè and dig into a freshly baked jam-filled croissant *(Piazza Brà 12, Verona • 045 803 1168)*.

A short stroll leads past the boutiques in traffic-free Via Mazzini, paved with pink-tinged local limestone embedded with ammonite fossils, to **Casa di Giulietta** to the right, or **Piazza delle Erbe** and its elegant palaces to the left.

Backtrack to Via Mazzini for lunch at Ristorante Greppia *(Vicolo Samaritana 3, Verona • 045 800 4577 • Closed Mon)* for bollito misto (nine types of boiled meat) served with a traditional peppery sauce.

Afternoon

To digest lunch, head over the Adige River via the ancient Ponte di Pietra to the Roman theatre on Via Regaste Redentore – well worth a visit even if you're not in town for a summer evening performance. Then follow the river or walk back through town and west towards the medieval Ponte Scaligero, part of the adjoining castle. The triple-arched construction was blown up by the German army in World War II, then rebuilt brick by brick by the town.

The bridge leads to Castelvecchio for a timely apéritif with a glass of white Soave wine at any of the welcoming bars.

Left **Villa Valmarana "Ai Nani"** Right **Villa Valmarana "La Rotonda"**

🔟 Veneto Villas

1 Villa Barbaro

The best preserved villa (1560) by Palladio *(see p45)* lies close to the pretty hilltown of Asolo. This charming country house features all manner of Roman-inspired elements, from the nymphaeum and grotto to the circular temple akin to the Pantheon. Playful *trompe l'oeil* frescoes by Veronese *(see p44)* adorn the main rooms alongside elaborate stucco work, while the garden is punctuated with Classical statuary. Drop in to the estate's wine cellar next door.

⌾ *Via Cornuda 6, Maser, bus from Treviso railway station • Open Mar–Oct: 3–6pm Tue, Sat, Sun & public hols; Nov–Feb: 2:30–5pm Sat, Sun & public hols • Admission charge*

2 Villa Pisani – La Nazionale

A splendid two-floor 18th-century villa designed for Doge Alvise Pisani, with 114 sumptuously furnished rooms and an impressive ballroom decorated by Tiepolo *(see p44)*. Above the huge façade columns, scores of statues line the roof overlooking inner courtyards and a spacious park where the Venetian nobility would promenade on summer evenings. Be sure to try out the wonderful 1721 circular maze. The guest list has included one-time proprietor Napoleon, Russian, Austrian and Swedish royalty, Mussolini and Hitler. ⌾ *Via Doge Pisani 7, Strà • Villa & park: open Apr–Sep: 9am–7pm Tue–Sun (Oct–Mar 9am–4pm); maze: open Apr–Oct • Admission charge*

3 Villa Valmarana "Ai Nani"

Known for the jaunty statues of dwarfs on the garden wall, these cosy twin buildings stand on a pretty ridge looking up to Monte Berico and its sanctuary. The Tiepolo father and son fresco team were invited here by Count Valmarana in 1757, the former to decorate the main part, the latter the Foresteria guest quarters. ⌾ *Via dei Nani 2–8, Vicenza • Open Mar–early Nov: 10am–noon, 3–6pm Tue–Sun; Nov–Feb: 10am–noon, 2–4pm Sat & Sun • Admission charge*

4 Villa Valmarana "La Rotonda"

Perfectly proportioned imposing villa with four temple façades on a hill overlooking the architect Palladio's adoptive town of Vicenza. The house has been imitated throughout the world. If you want to visit the gilded stuccoed and domed villa as opposed to the rather limited grounds, time your visit carefully as it's only open one day per week. ⌾ *Via Rotonda 29, Vicenza (bus No. 8) • Open 15 Mar–4 Nov: garden 10am–noon, 3–6pm Tue–Sun (5 Nov–mid-Mar: 10am–noon, 2:30–5pm); villa 10am–noon, 3–6pm Wed • Admission charge*

5 Villa Foscari "La Malcontenta"

Wonderful dignified residence set on the bend of the Brenta Canal, though now rather too close to the Marghera industrial area. Designed by Andrea Palladio in 1571, it is one of his

Left **Villa Foscari** Right **Villa Emo**

most famous creations, with a Greek temple façade, while the interior glows with allegorical frescoes. The name is a reference to the "discontent" of a female member of the Foscari family, exiled here for adultery. ◉ *Via dei Turisti 11, Malcontenta • Open Apr–Oct: 9am–noon Tue, Sat • Admission charge*

Villa Barbarigo
The Euganean Hills are the perfect setting for this Baroque garden, designed for the Barbarigo family from Venice by Luigi Bernini, architect of the Vatican fountains in Rome. The villa, dating from 1669, is a private dwelling, but the 15-ha (37-acre) garden provides a boxwood maze, fountains, fish ponds, statues and hundreds of trees. ◉ *Galzignano, Valsanzibio • Open Mar–Nov: 10am–1pm, 2pm–sunset daily • Admission charge*

Villa Emo
Another of Palladio's light-flooded country residences, this one was commissioned by the Emo family and built around 1560. A harmonious central block is flanked by graceful arched *barchesse* (wings), designed for storing hay and farm tools. The interior has lively frescoes by Renaissance artist Zelotti, also responsible for the Malcontenta villa decorations. ◉ *Via Stazione 5, Fanzolo di Vedelago • Open Mar–Oct: 3–7pm Mon–Sat, 10am–12:30pm, 3–7pm Sun & public hols; Nov–Feb: 1–4:30pm Mon–Fri, 1:30–5pm Sat, Sun & hols • Admission charge*

Villa Contarini
A horseshoe plaza lined with terraced houses faces the façade of this 17th-century country villa, once the focus for a thriving farming community. A remarkable system of acoustics was invented so that musicians performing in the Sala della Musica on the first floor could be clearly appreciated downstairs. An antiques market is held in the grounds on the last Sunday of each month.
◉ *Piazzola sul Brenta • Open Mar–Oct: 9am–7pm daily; Nov–Feb: 10am–4pm Tue–Sun • Admission charge*

Villa Cornaro
Unusual double-tiered, compact Palladio creation, this one dates back to 1560–70. The façade columns are both Corinthian and Doric in style, with acanthus leaves or scrolls around the capitals.
◉ *Via Roma 34, Piombino Dese • Open May–Sep: 3:30–6pm Sat • Admission charge*

Barchessa Valmarana
Formerly guest quarters, these are extant "wings" of a 17th-century villa, whose main body was demolished in 1908. Close by are locks on the Brenta waterway, which have been excavated over centuries to divert the river away from the lagoon and eliminate the problem of silting. ◉ *Via Valmarana 11, Mira Porte • Open Mar–Oct: 10am–6pm • Admission charge*

Left **Cappelleria Palladio** Right **Mercato d'Oriente**

Veneto Shops

1 Pasticceria Forin

A pastry shop specializing in biscuits named after St Anthony and studded with pistachios, pine nuts and marsala. The *pièce de résistance* is a large bun shaped to resemble the town's domed basilica and flavoured with *amaretto* (almond liqueur). ⊗ *Via S Francesco 179, Padua*

2 Drogheria ai Due Catini D'Oro

An old-fashioned shop selling super strong mints, peppery Veneto *mostarda* chutney and even feather dusters. ⊗ *Piazza dei Frutti, Padua*

3 Feltrinelli Internazionale

Browse through the well-stocked shelves of English- and other European-language crime and mystery novels, fiction, travel, classics, children's literature and reference books in this chain bookshop. ⊗ *Via S Francesco 14, Padua*

4 Antica Pasticceria di Sorarù

Inviting pastry shop lined with tantalizing almond and chocolate delicacies, and special goodies such as the dove-shaped *Colomba* cake at Easter. ⊗ *Piazzetta Palladio 17, Vicenza*

5 Cappelleria Palladio

Hat-lovers' heaven, run by a charming couple with a 40-year passion for millinery in this lovely old-fashioned establishment. In great demand for stylish weddings in the country villas *(see pp126–7)*. ⊗ *Piazzetta Palladio 13, Vicenza*

6 Il Ceppo

A gourmet's paradise with mouth-watering take-away dishes, pickles and preserves. Buy a catered picnic with wine or simply a crusty roll filled with Asiago cheese or *sopressa* sausage. ⊗ *Corso Palladio 196, Vicenza*

7 De Rossi "Il Fornaio"

A range of pastries and wholemeal breads. Try the *zaletto*, a biscuit baked with pine nuts and sultanas, and of course *Baci di Giulietta* (Juliet's Kisses) – almond paste shaped into pursed lips. ⊗ *Corso Porta Borsari 3, Verona*

8 Love Therapy – Elio Fiorucci

Colourful fun fashion accessories and gadgets alongside top-brand clothing. ⊗ *Via Mazzini 6, Verona*

9 Mercato d'Oriente

Akin to an exotic museum, this antiques dealer dazzles with Chinese and Japanese marvels, Pre-Columbian pieces and both traditional and contemporary carpets. ⊗ *Corso S Anastasia 34, Verona*

10 Upim

Wonderful department store with a good range of casual clothes, cosmetics and home furnishings, in the centre of town. ⊗ *Via Mazzini 6, Verona*

Around Town – Padua, Vicenza & Verona

For more on shopping in Venice **See p138**

Left **Caffè Pedrocchi** Right **Caffè Dante Ristoratore**

🔟 Places to Eat

Graziati

Buttery *millefoglie* pastries
perfectly accompany a strong
sweet coffee as you sit outside
on the lively market square. Light
lunches are served downstairs.
◈ *Piazza della Frutta 40, Padua • €*

Caffè Pedrocchi

This 1831 Neo-Classical
coffee house was long known as
the "café without doors"
because it never closed. Liberals
of the 19th century would meet
and argue here, though today,
after a renovation, it's rather
quiet. ◈ *Via VIII Febbraio 15, Padua • €*

Osteria dei Fabbri

The appetizing menu in this
rustic *osteria* changes daily, so
you may get grilled Piedmont
cheese with polenta or spare ribs
with *radicchio*. ◈ *Via dei Fabbri 13,
Padua • 049 650 3362 • Closed Sun • €€*

Osteria al Bersagliere

This refined *osteria* does
variations on the area's seasonal
cuisine. A local favourite is
Baccalà alla Vicentina, dried salt
cod stewed in milk. ◈ *Via Pescaria
11, Vicenza • 044 432 3507 • Closed Sun
• No disabled access • €€*

Antica Casa della Malvasia

A restaurant with an imaginative
menu and a vast wine list. Try
the *Bigoli all'arna* (spaghetti with
duck sauce). ◈ *Contrada Morette 5,
Vicenza • 044 454 3704 • Closed Mon,
2 weeks Aug • €*

Self Pause

At the western end of the
main street, this great self-
service restaurant offers cheap,
tasty salads, pasta and meat
dishes and a great value buffet
for dinner. ◈ *Corso A Palladio 10,
Vicenza • 044 327829 • Closed Sun L • €*

Pizzeria Bella Vicenza

Just off the main square,
this great-value pizzeria proudly
specializes in seasonal vegetable
toppings, such as peas, asparagus, aubergine (eggplant) or red
chicory. ◈ *Contrà dei Proti 12, Vicenza
• 044 454 6192 • Closed Mon D, Tue • No
disabled access • €*

Caffè Dante Ristoratore

This stylish café can be
found in a quiet historic square
surrounded by graceful palaces.
The place to be seen, sipping tea
amid potted palms and cane
chairs. ◈ *Piazza dei Signori, Verona*

Brek

Right across from the Arena,
this well-reputed self-service
Italian chain restaurant offers a
vast variety of meats, cheeses
and vegetable dishes. ◈ *Piazza Brà
20, Verona • 045 800 4561 • €*

Bottega del Vino

Renowned restaurant that
dates back to 1890 and holds
2,500 wines in its cellar. Food-
wise, the favourite is *pastissada
de caval*, a spicy stew. ◈ *Vicolo
Scudo di Francia 3, Verona • 045 800 4535
• Closed Tue out of opera season • €€€*

 Note: *Unless otherwise stated, all restaurants accept credit
cards and serve vegetarian meals*

STREETSMART

VENICE'S TOP 10

Left **International Student Card** Centre **Sunbathing, the Lido** Right **Airline ticket**

Planning Your Trip

1 What to Pack

Comfortable walking shoes, boots or sandals are essential. You'll be on your feet for a good part of your visit and the stone paving can prove tiring. Bring a bag or case on wheels so that it is easy to get on and off boats and ferries.

2 Passports, Visas and ID Cards

A passport with a minimum five months validity is necessary for nationals of all countries entering Italy. For residents of the EU, USA, Canada, Australia and New Zealand, visas are only required for stays exceeding three months or for those intending to work, but it is always advisable to check with your embassy before travelling. Students should bring an International Student Card (ISIC) for reduced admission fees.

3 Driving Licence

If you plan on any out-of-Venice trips with a rented car, bring a valid driving licence and credit card. Residents from outside the EU will need an International Driver's Licence. If driving your own car, bring vehicle registration papers and full insurance cover. Italians drive on the right.

4 Children's Needs

Young children tire quickly and a fold-up stroller is essential. A backpack child carrier can be worth its weight in gold and can double as a high chair, which are rare in Venice restaurants.

5 When to Go

There's no such thing as a "bad" time to visit Venice. Every season has its attractions, whether that be hot summer days with balmy evenings; melancholic autumn with its fog; crisp winter with the snow-bound Alps as a backdrop, or mild spring with its photogenic sunsets.

6 Public Holidays

In addition to those recognized throughout Italy *(see box)*, the Venice Salute festivity falls on 21 November *(see p62)* and St Mark's Day on 25 April.

7 Time Difference

Italy is one hour ahead of Greenwich Mean Time (GMT), meaning London is one hour behind Venice, the US Eastern Seaboard six hours behind, while most of Australia is nine hours ahead and Japan eight hours ahead. Italy changes to Daylight Saving Time *(ora legale)* from the last Sunday in March through to the last Sunday in October, moving the time difference to GMT plus two hours.

8 Sun Protection

Sunglasses, protective cream and a hat are essential from spring to autumn for pale complexions. Don't underestimate the strength of the sun and remember that there is added reflection from the water.

9 Insect Repellent

Mosquitoes and gnats are a nuisance in summer and few hotels or apartments have protective screening. Should you forget your own, pharmacies stock a wide range of repellents in liquid and electrical form.

10 Electrical Appliances

Italian plugs and sockets entail two or three round prongs and electricity is 220V AC. If you envisage using any appliances

Mosquito repellent and Italian plug

with you, as they're all but unheard of in Venice.

Public Holidays

New Year's Day (1 Jan)
Epiphany (6 Jan)
Easter Monday (variable)
Liberation Day (25 Apr)
Labour Day (1 May)
Republic Day (2 June)
Assumption (15 Aug)
All Saints' Day (1 Nov)
Immaculate Conception (8 Dec)
Christmas Day (25 Dec)
Boxing Day (26 Dec).

Left **Venice Marco Polo Airport** Centre **Arriving by boat** Right **Tronchetto car park**

Arriving in Venice

1 Venice Airport

Marco Polo Airport is located at Tessera, 8 km (5 miles) north of the city, on the edge of the lagoon, so arrivals and departures are scenic affairs. Many European airlines serve the airport including British Airways and low cost Easyjet. Visitors from outside Europe need to fly to Rome or Milan for connecting flights to Venice. ⊗ Flight information:041 260 9240
• www.veniceairport.it

2 Water Connections

The most exciting way to reach Venice from the airport is by water – the frequent Alilaguna ferries charge about €10. A private water taxi, however, will set you back an vast amount (around €90), depending on time of day and the amount of baggage you have (see p135).

3 Road Connections

To go as far as Piazzale Roma, Venice's car and bus terminal, the cheapest option is the orange ACTV bus No. 5 (see p135), every 20 minutes during the day. Tickets are available from newsagents. Or there's the direct ATVO blue bus (tickets available in the arrivals hall).

4 Treviso Airport

Ryanair flies into Treviso airport from the UK and a special bus transports passengers to and from Venice (45 minutes). The airport can also be reached by train from Venice to Treviso, then local bus No. 6, although this route does take longer.
⊗ 0422 315 111 • www. trevisoairport.it

5 By Train

Don't make the mistake of many first-time visitors and get off at Venezia Mestre, but wait until the train has crossed the lagoon for Venezia Santa Lucia Station. The Orient Express is an expensive but memorable way to travel from London between March and November.
⊗ Train timetables: 892021
• www.trenitalia.com
• www.orient-express.com

6 By Road

Whether you zoom in to the city via the motorway (autostrada) or on minor roads, you'll need to follow signs for "Venezia". Long-distance buses arrive in Venice at Piazzale Roma.
⊗ Road conditions information:1518 • ACI (Italian Automobile Club) breakdown service: 803116

7 Car Parking

The Tronchetto island car park has bus and boat links to the rest of Venice, otherwise it's Piazzale Roma for the exorbitant garages (parcheggio). A more reasonable option is

Serenissima opposite the railway station in Mestre. The car park and boat terminal at Fusina on the eastern edge of the lagoon is also handy. Despite the expense of car parks, never resort to roadside parking – car break-ins are all too common in the area.

8 By Sea

Daily car and passenger ferries arrive from Greece across the Adriatic and dock at the San Basilio terminal in western Dorsoduro (see p93), equipped with an information office and catering facilities. It also acts as the jump-off point for week-long cruises to the Greek Islands.

9 Porters

Porters (portabagagli) equipped with trolleys and broad shoulders can usually be found at the maritime passenger terminal, railway station, airport, bus terminal and car park, and at strategic points around town such as Rialto and Piazza San Marco. Rates start at around €16 per item.

10 Left Luggage

Lockers and a left luggage office (deposito bagagli) function at Santa Lucia railway station and Marco Polo airport. The Piazzale Roma bus terminal also has a convenient left luggage facility located next to the Pullman Bar.

Left **Concert poster** Centre left **Ospite di Venezia** Centre right and right **Italian tourist office logos**

🔟 Sources of Information

1 Tourist Offices in Venice
There are numerous helpful tourist offices around the city *(see box)*.

2 Tourist Offices in the Veneto
Each of the main towns in the Veneto has a tourist information office *(see box)*.

3 AVA Venice Hoteliers' Association
For a modest fee, hotel bookings can be made at a number of AVA offices. ❀ Airport: 041 541 5017 • Piazzale Roma Garage Comunale: 041 522 8640 • Piazzale Roma Garage San Marco: 041 523 1397 • Ferrovia: 041 715 288 • Tronchetto: 041 528 7833

4 Last-Minute Reservations
The efficient VeneziaSì booking service run by the Hoteliers' Association can arrange accommodation on the spur of the moment, free of charge. ❀ 800 843 006 (freephone within Italy) • 041 522 2264 (from abroad) • www. veneziasi.it • info@ veneziasi.it

5 Ospite di Venezia
This excellent free magazine published every month in English (as *Guest in Venice*) and Italian by the Hoteliers' Association is distributed at hotels. Crammed with practical details, boat timetables and info on exhibitions and concerts.

6 Wall Posters
Many events in Venice are announced at the last minute by eye-catching posters along the main streets or small versions in shop windows. Get in the habit of reading them for all manner of fascinating local festivities and cultural events.

7 Leo
The Venice Tourist Board's complimentary glossy three-monthly publication has a detachable pocket-sized programme of exhibitions, concerts and events. Request it for free at tourist offices.

8 Venezia da Vivere
Aimed at young visitors, this slim, brightly coloured booklet printed quarterly by the City Council contains listings of what's on, live music, poetry readings, cheap places to eat and shop. You can pick up a copy in bars and shops.

9 Pocket Venice
Another useful free three-monthly bilingual magazine that lists exhibitions, not to mention bars and eateries all around town.

10 Websites
As well as the Tourist Board sites *(see box)*, www.meeting venice.it and www.a guestinvenice.com in Italian and English are excellent sources of information and have an incredible number and array of useful links for in-depth exploration.

Tourist Offices

Venice
www.turismovenezia.it
• 041 529 8711

Ferrovia S Lucia (railway station)
• 041 529 8727

Piazza S Marco 71/f
• 041 529 8740

Venice Pavilion
• Giardinetti Reali, S Marco 2
• 041 522 5150

Piazzale Roma, Garage Comunale
• 041 529 8746

Airport • 041 541 5887

Gran Viale 6, Lido
• 041 526 5721 (summer only)

Padua
Piazzale della Stazione
• 049 875 2077
• www.turismopadova.it

Vicenza
Piazza Matteotti 12
• 044 432 0854
• www.vicenzae.org

Verona
Via degli Alpini 9
• 045 806 8680
• www.tourism.verona.it

Left **Venice street signs** Centre **Gondola ride** Right **Vaporetto arriving at San Marco**

🔟 Getting Around Venice

1 Asking Directions
Whatever your request, a Venetian will nearly always answer "*sempre diritto*" ("straight on"). The idea is that by following the main flow of pedestrians you'll reach the main sights. A detailed map is always a good idea.

2 Street Signs
Yellow placards point visitors in the direction of the main landmarks such as San Marco, Rialto, Ferrovia (railway station) and Piazzale Roma (bus terminal and car park). But be aware that inconsistencies in spelling may be encountered between street signs and addresses in this guide due to the Venetian dialect applied to local names.

3 Boat Lines
The ACTV runs a marvellous network of public ferries throughout Venice and the lagoon. Buy your ticket beforehand or, if the landing stage is unmanned, ask the crew for a ticket as soon as you board.
🕲 www.actv.it(for routes and timetables)

4 Boat Fares
A one-way ticket can be expensive (around €5 along the Grand Canal). You can get better value from a 24-hour or 72-hour ticket (€10.50 and €22). Children under four years of age travel free on all public transport.

5 Island Boat Fares
A *laguna nord* day ticket is a good deal for the panoramic circuit via Murano, Burano and its neighbours, as well as Punta Sabbioni (see pp108–111). An equivalent applies for the Lido-Chioggia route (see pp114–17) via a combination of buses and ferries.

6 Season Tickets
If you're staying longer than a few weeks, it's worth investing in an *abbonamento* (travel pass). A passport-sized photo is required. Apply to ACTV/Vela at Piazzale Roma.

7 Gondolas
Charges are around €73 for 50 minutes with a maximum of six passengers, although this increases after 8pm. The gondola *traghetto* ferry service across the Grand Canal is far cheaper if less romantic (see p22).

8 Water Taxis
Not exactly a cheap transport option, but it's undeniably stylish to cruise around in a varnished waterborne equivalent of a limousine if you can afford it (see p22).
🕲 Consorzio Motoscafi: 041 522 2303 • Serenissima: 041 522 8538

9 Combined City Museum Ticket
The €15.50 Musei Civici ticket covers entrance to the Doge's Palace (see pp12–15), Museo Correr including the archaeological section and Libreria Sansovino (see p18), Ca' Pesaro (see p41), Palazzo Mocenigo (see p82), the Glass and Lace museums (see pp40–41) and Ca' Rezzonico (see p21). The pass is excellent value.

10 Chorus Church Pass
If you plan on visiting most of the 15 outstanding churches managed by the Chorus organization, splash out on the all-inclusive combined ticket, rather than paying admission charges for each one. Included among the churches are Santa Maria Gloriosa dei Frari (see pp26–7), Santa Maria dei Miracoli, San Sebastiano and Madonna dell'Orto (see pp38–9). 🕲 Chorus: 041 275 0462 • www.chorusvenezia.org

Ca' Pesaro museum

➡ For Venice's watercraft **See pp22–3**

Left **Official Venice tour guide** Right **Gondola serenade**

Guided Tours

1 Official Tour Guides

The city's certified multi-lingual guides, catering for individuals and groups, cover every corner of Venice with in-depth history and history of art explanations in some 15 different languages.
◉ Calle Morosini della Regina, S Marco 750 • 041 520 9038 • www.guidevenezia.it

2 American Express

An attractive range of walking and gondola sightseeing tours accompanied by qualified English-speaking guides takes place daily. They last for around two hours.
◉ Salizzada S Moisè, S Marco 1471 • 041 520 0844 • www.americanexpress.it

3 Gondola Serenades

If you can't afford a gondola all for yourself, then a group cruise along the romantic canals serenaded by a baritone singing "O sole mio!" is a must. Reservations can be made through travel agents around the city or ask at the gondoliers' stands.

4 Island Boat trips

The outlying islands of Murano, Burano (see pp108–111) and Torcello (see pp30–31) are visited on a four-hour trip in sleek motor launches with a multilingual guide (9:30am and 2:30pm Apr–Oct, 2pm Nov–Mar).

Book your ticket at a travel agency or at kiosks in Piazza San Marco.

5 Museum Tours

To get the most out of your visit, join a guided tour run by expert English-speaking staff in the city's many superb museums. Particularly good recommendations are those at the Archaeological Museum and Sala Sansovino (see p18). Most tours have no extra charge, although a small fee is payable at the Accademia Galleries (see pp24–5) and the Doge's Palace (see pp12–15).

6 Doge's Palace "Secret Itineraries" Tour

In addition to the official parts of the Doge's Palace, these tours take you "behind the scenes", and come complete with fascinating historical anecdotes. Advance booking recommended (see pp12–15).

7 Brenta Villas

This leisurely if rather exorbitantly priced full-day ferry trip across the lagoon sails via the locks on the Brenta Canal to visit a selection of stately villas, once summer residences of the Venetian nobility. Return is by bus. It is run by Il Burchiello in Padua, but can also be booked via Venice travel agents.
◉ Il Burchiello: SITA, Via Orlandini 3, Padua

• 049 820 6910
• www.ilburchiello.it
• end Mar–Oct: Venice to Padua Tue, Thu & Sat; Padua to Venice Wed, Fri & Sun

8 Wagner's Room, Casino

The premises where the German romantic composer Richard Wagner wrote operas, and ultimately passed away, can be visited with an expert multilingual guide at 10:30am.
◉ Booking essential Fri 10am–noon • 349 593 6990 • Donation (minimum €5)

9 Venice Walks

Themed walking tours led by experts are an intriguing way to get to know Venice. Some of the possibilities include visiting the haunts of well-known ghosts, taking in the art and architecture of the city, or discovering some of Venice's most beautiful gardens. Alternatively, take a flight over the lagoon or the Dolomites for a more expensive and less strenuous option.
◉ Frezzaria, S Marco 1827 • 041 523 9979 • www.veniceevents.com

10 Jewish Ghetto

Expert guides take you to old synagogues hidden away amidst a maze of rooms and cramped floors in the fascinating Ghetto and its layers of history (see p95).

Left **Venice market** Centre **Litorale del Cavallino camping ground** Right **Venice sales sign**

🔟 Venice on a Budget

1 Rolling Venice
A handy pass for 14–29-year-olds entailing holders to a boat/bus ticket that lasts 72 hours, and a range of discounts on hotels, restaurants and shops. It is available either from main ACTV/ Vela ticket offices *(see p135)*, Tourist Info *(see p134)*, or from the Rolling Venice office. ◈ *Rolling Venice: Rio Terrà dei Pensieri, S Croce 365/A • 041 272 7225*

2 Accommodation
Sleep cheaply in Venice itself at one of several hostels, otherwise use the camp sites on the mainland or the beach areas – there are cabins or caravans if you don't have a tent *(see p151)*. Crashing out at the railway station is often tolerated though not particularly safe.

3 Public Transport
You can save money by just walking everywhere, unless you're staying at the Giudecca hostel or want to visit the islands. Rather than expensive singles, the boat passes *(see p135)* or Rolling Venice special deal are recommended.

4 Picnic Supplies
There are wonderful produce markets at Rialto *(see pp28–9)*, Rio Terrà San Leonardo, Campo Santa Margherita *(see pp32–3)* and Via Garibaldi, while supermarkets Co-

op, SU.VE and Billa are dotted all over town. Cheap wine is dispensed by the litre *(vino sfuso)* at the many Nave de Oro outlets – take a plastic bottle.

5 Eating out
Italian-style fast food is on at Brek *(see p99)* or hamburgers at Burger King *(see p65)* and McDonald's *(see p78)*. For more substantial fare seek out a *tavola calda* where hot meals are served at the counter and customers sit on stools. Another option is the set tourist menu *(menu turistico)* in restaurants.

6 Concessions
Children and students with an ISIC (International Students Card) are not the only ones eligible for entry concessions: senior citizens should always enquire at council and state-run museums.

7 Italian Culture Week
Entrance to state-run museums and galleries is free of charge throughout Italy for the *Settimana della cultura*, usually in late February or March.

8 Cheap Rail Fares
Several good-value rail fares may be on offer throughout the year. Book online at www. trenitalia.com or enquire at the station or travel agencies bearing the FS logo. To travel cheaply avoid the ES and IC trains which entail hefty supplements, and go for the IR and R slower trains.

9 Shopping
Venice's suburb of Mestre is worth a visit for clothing, shoes and accessories at lower prices than in the city. It also has a huge market on Wednesday and Friday mornings.

10 Orange Laundry
Save on hotel laundry bills by using this self-service laundrette which guarantees a 45-minute turn-around time. ◈ *Campiello delle Muneghe, S Croce 6650B*

Venetian grocery shop, San Marco

Left **Venetian market** Centre **Mask selection** Right **Street stall**

🔟 Shopping Tips

1 Opening Hours
Food shops open
Monday to Saturday
around 8–9am, take a
long lunch break and
then resume business
5–7:30pm, except for
Wednesday afternoon
when most are closed. In
low season clothing and
other shops usually close
all day Sunday and
Monday morning. Glass
furnaces (see p64) do not
often give demonstra-
tions at weekends.

2 Sales
The official periods
for sales (saldi) are mid-
January to mid-February
then late July to late
August. Retailers must
show the item's original
cost alongside the sale
price so customers know
how much they're saving.
Vendita promozionale is
another term for a sale.

**3 Tax-Free
Shopping**
Visitors from non-EU
countries can claim a tax
refund on purchases that
exceed €155 from the
one shop. Most shop-
keepers will have the
appropriate forms –
check for the relevant
window sticker first.

4 Bargaining
Centuries of
commerce have shaped
the Venetians into die-
hard traders, who feign
offence when discounts
(sconti) are requested
but it's worth a try for
cash transactions.

**5 Where to Buy
Gourmet Delights**
Delicatessens and
specialist shops are clus-
tered around the Rialto
market (see pp28–9),
with fresh buffalo
mozzarella from the
south of Italy, unusual
pasta and all manner of
delectable ready-to-eat
dishes. Supermarkets are
also worth perusing for
bottled treats.

**6 Where to Buy
English Books**
As well as the Pavilion
Bookshop (see p69) and
the Libreria Giunti (see
p98), novels and guide
books in English and
other languages can also
be found at Libreria
Goldoni and Libreria
Mondadori. ◈ Libreria
Goldoni: Calle dei Fabbri, S
Marco 4742 041 522 2384 •
Libreria Mondadori
Salizzada San Moisè, San
Marco 1345 041 522 2193

Venice street seller

**7 Where to Buy
Glassware**
It's worth shopping
around as many glass
shops stock similar items
and prices can vary
wildly. Murano (see p109)
tends to be more
expensive than Venice
but you get a free
demonstration as well.

8 Hypermarkets
Free shuttle buses
leave the Piazzale Roma
terminal at regular
intervals for the huge
mainland shopping
centres of Panorama,
located at Marghera,
Carrefour at Marcon and
Auchan on the outskirts
of Mestre. They're good
for everything from
groceries through to
computers, clothing and
sports gear.

9 Street Sellers
Pavement trading is
brisk in tourist bric-à-brac
as well as imitation
designer bags and
accessories, with
bargaining the name of the
game. However foreign
visitors should be warned
that hefty fines are
imposed for counterfeit
goods (see p140).

**10 Forwarding
Goods Home**
Virtually all glass shop
staff are experts in
packaging fragile and
bulky items and they can
arrange for forwarding
overseas by air or sea.
Always check that
insurance is included.

For more shops in Venice See pp68–9

Left **Disabled accessibility sign** Centre and right **Wheelchair ramps in Venice**

Venice for the Disabled

1 Maps
Ask at tourist offices (see p134) for the special map of Venice which shows areas and bridges accessible for wheelchairs clearly highlighted in yellow.

2 Bridges
Cannaregio's Ponte delle Guglie has been fitted with a low stepped if rather steep ramp, while four in the San Marco district have a mechanized stair-climber (Ponte Goldoni, Ponte Manin, Ponte del Teatro, Ponte dei Frati). The necessary key is available at tourist offices and must be returned.

3 Hotels
Apart from the luxury chains, few hotels in Venice have wheelchair facilities let alone ele-vators, mainly due to renovation restrictions on historic buildings (which covers virtually every-thing in town). However a ground-floor room

(camera a piano terra) may be feasible. Addresses can be found in Tourism for all in the Veneto (see "Local Contact" below). The Venice tourist office has a brochure of suitable available accommodation.

4 Restaurants
Luckily the majority are located on the ground floor though they are not necessarily spacious. Outside dining usually offers easier access.

5 Buses
ACTV bus No. 5, which runs between Piaz-zale Roma and the airport, is fitted with a mobile platform for wheelchairs and a reserved space with safety straps.

6 Boats
The ACTV vaporetto has a spacious flat area and is easy to get on and off as the landing stages are on the same level as the passenger deck. The motoscafo is best avoided. The Alilaguna

launch to and from the airport (see p133) is also wheelchair accessible.

7 Taxis
Waterborne taxis are out of the question unless you can handle steps. However Sanitrans, an efficient private ambulance/taxi service can be booked. The Cooperativa San Marco also has special craft though at a higher rate.
⊛ Sanitrans:041 513 9977
• Consorzio Motoscafi: 041 240 67 11

8 Public Conveniences
The main public toilets in Venice are accessible to disabled users.

9 Local Contact
The helpful council-run Informahandicap in Mestre can answer enquiries and assist disabled visitors to Venice. ⊛ Informahandicap: Centro Culturale Candiani, Piazza Candiani 5, Mestre 041 274 6144 • www.comune.venezia.it/informahandicap

10 Airline and Train Travel
When booking your flight make a request for assis-tance both on board and at the airport. For trains, railway personnel can aid wheelchair users with a special elevator. Notice of 24 hours is necessary for Italian and international rail travel. ⊛ Italian Rail: 199 303060

Mechanized wheelchair-climber on a Venetian bridge

Left **Queues for Basilica San Marco** Right **Travelling by vaporetto**

TOP 10 Things to Avoid

1 Bringing Too Much Luggage
Firstly because it will be a hindrance in this carless city (you will have to carry it yourself) and secondly because you'll want space for souvenirs.

2 Sticking to the Beaten Track
If you veer away from the signposted – and crowded – triangle between Rialto, San Marco and Accademia, you will most likely find yourself on some deserted but charming canals and get a glimpse of real Venetian life.

3 Clogging up the Streets
People keep to the right here. This habit is of special importance in narrow crowded alleyways to ensure pedestrian flow, not to mention when you're negotiating the raised walkways when the city is flooded.

4 Smoking
By law, restaurants, offices and all public premises throughout Italy are all non-smoking indoors. This prohibition is taken seriously and fines are fairly hefty!

5 Scams
The Tronchetto Island car park is akin to a "jungle". Don't believe anyone who claims to be a parking attendant (there aren't any) and don't pre-pay a "return" boat ride to your hotel. In Venice itself, don't fall for the "three boxes" betting trick which goes on illegally on bridges.

6 Hidden Costs
Whether ordering a meal or taking a taxi or gondola, it's a good rule to verify all charges beforehand to avoid nasty surprises. Complaints can be addressed to the Tourist Board (041 529 8710 or complaint.apt@turismovenezia.it). Tipping *(la mancia)* in restaurants is at your own discretion as a service charge *(servizio)* is generally included.

7 Buying Goods Without a Receipt
Shopkeepers are obliged to provide customers with a receipt by law and it's also needed if you later decide to exchange an item and for customs when you leave.

8 Entering Churches in Beachwear
Catholic churches no longer require visitors to cover their head, but do still outlaw beachwear, shorts, T-shirts and photographs. Remember, they are still places of worship as well as art galleries.

9 Counterfeit Design Goods
It is important to remember that both the customer and the vendor can be fined up to €10,000 for dealing in fake designer items, such as the handbags which are readily available on the streets.

10 Getting Stranded
Venice isn't a huge city, but travelling by *vaporetto* can be slow. Allow plenty of transit time to reach the station to catch a train or to keep an appointment.

Alcohol in moderation is part of Venetian life

Left **Public telephone sign** Right **Browsing at a newsstand**

Banking & Communications

Currency
In January 2002 Italy joined 11 other European countries by converting its currency to the euro. As a result, the Italian lira was phased out from 1 July 2002. Euro banknotes, which can be used throughout 12 EC countries, have seven denominations: 5, 10, 20, 50, 100, 200 and 500. There are also eight coin denominations: 2 euros and 1 euro, and 50, 20, 10, 5, 2 and 1 cents. Check on exchange rates against your own currency at the time of travel.

Cash Dispensers (ATMs)
Cashpoints are plentiful all over Venice, usually outside bank premises, and allow you to withdraw money around the clock. The logos of the cards accepted are on display. Automatic currency exchange machines with multilingual instructions can also be found in key tourist points.

Credit Cards
The most convenient way to carry money and a great help in an emergency. All the major credit cards (MasterCard, Visa, American Express) are widely accepted in restaurants, shops, hotels, and can also be used to obtain a cash advance. Diner's Card is often quoted as the unwanted exception.

Travellers' Cheques
Choose a well-known company such as Visa or Thomas Cook, a major currency such as sterling or US dollars, and high denominations as a commission is payable for each transaction. You need to show identification to cash cheques. Keep the receipt and a note of serial numbers separate from the cheques in case of loss. Travellers' cheques in euros are increasingly available.

Changing Money
Exchange offices are abundant and usually keep long hours, weekends and public holidays included. Compared to banks they demand a higher commission and give a slightly lower rate but they mean less paperwork and shorter queues. It's worth shopping around to compare rates. Post offices also have exchange facilities.

Post Offices
The main Rialto GPO is open Monday to Saturday, 8:30am–6:30pm, the branch on Lista di Spagna, Monday to Friday 8:30am–2pm, Saturday 8:30am–1pm, as is the one off Piazza San Marco. Stamps are also sold at tobacconists displaying a black-and-white "T" sign. Air mail has been replaced with *Posta Prioritaria* for a faster service.

Internet
Internet points have mushroomed in Venice and range from cramped single-computer affairs to flashy modern premises such as InternetPoint (extended opening hours). Budget hotels are now installing e-mail points as well.
Ⓢ *InternetPoint: Campo S Stefano, S Marco 2967-2968 • Map M5*

Post Office sign

Telephones
There's a public phone on every corner in Venice and pre-paid phonecards *(scheda telefonica)* are sold at tobacconists; remove the dotted corner before use. Dial the zero of all area codes.

Press
Newsstands at hot spots such as the railway station and Rialto sell *Time* magazine, several UK newspapers such as *the Guardian*, and the *International Herald Tribune*.

TV
Increasing numbers of hotels provide satellite TV for guests so English-language stations, such as CNN, BBC World Service and Sky News, are common.

Left **Policemen in Venice** Right **Crowds of tourists**

 Security & Health

1 Police

Two police forces operate in Italy. The blue-uniformed *polizia* answer freephone 113 emergency calls, while the military *carabinieri* in red-and-black gear respond to law and order problems on freephone 112. Thefts and serious problems can be reported to either force. ✆ *Polizia: Fondamenta S Lorenzo, Castello 5053, Map F3 • Carabinieri: Campo S Zaccaria, Castello 4693/A, Map F4*

2 Pickpockets

Street crime is relatively unusual in Venice but by no means lacking. Pickpockets prey on tourists in crowded places, notably Piazza San Marco and on waterbuses. Put valuables in the hotel safe if possible and don't keep any on show.

3 Consulates and Embassies

Venice itself does not have major embassies in the city apart from the UK consulate, but the nearest Italian consulates and embassies will be able to assist *(see box)*.

4 Lost Credit Cards and Travellers' Cheques

The minute you realize either are missing report it to the relevant number. ✆ *Visa: freephone 800 877232 (cards and cheques) • American Express: 067 228 03 71*

(cards); 800 872000 (cheques) • Thomas Cook: freephone 800 872050 (cheques)

5 Women Travellers

Dangerous situations are unusual in Venice as the main streets are rarely empty. However keep away from the Lido beaches at night and stick to busy areas. Chatting up foreign women continues to be a popular pastime for Venetian men.

6 Health Insurance

Visitors from EU countries should be equipped with a European Health Insurance Card (EHIC) to avoid emergency fees. Australia also has a reciprocal health agreement with Italy so the appropriate paperwork is needed. All other nationalities should take out private health insurance.

7 Pharmacies

Seek advice at a pharmacy *(farmacia)* to treat a minor ailment – English is widely understood. Outside shop hours check the pharmacy's door or the local paper *Il Gazzettino* for the night pharmacy roster.

Pharmacy sign

8 Hospitals

Pronto soccorso is the round-the-clock casualty department in hospitals *(ospedale)*, whose staff are usually familiar with the main European languages. Venice's main hospital is the Ospedale Civile. ✆ *Campo SS Giovanni e Paolo • Map R2*

9 Ambulances

Telephone 118 (free call) anywhere in Italy for an ambulance, including a waterborne *ambulanza* in Venice. Give the name of a prominent landmark nearby to help them locate you.

10 Public Conveniences

These are signposted with a blue-green-white WC logo and are open daily 8/9am–7/8pm and cost around 50 cents.

Consulates & Embassies

Australia
Via Antonio Bosio 5, Rome • 06 852 721
Canada
Via Vittor Pisani 19, Milan • 0267 581
New Zealand
Via Zara 28, Rome • 06 441 7171
United Kingdom
Piazzale Donatori Sangue 2, Mestre • 041 5055 990
United States
Via Principe Amadeo 2/10, Milan • 02 290 351

Left **Restoration workshop** Right **Glassblowing techniques**

Studying in Venice

1 Art Courses
Atmospheric studio that offers tuition in sculpture, watercolours, printing techniques and drawing, both short and long term. ◈ *Bottega del Tintoretto, Fondamenta dei Mori, Cannaregio 3400* • *041 722 081* • *www. tintorettovenezia.it*

2 University Italian Language Courses
The Ca' Foscari University's language centre offers semi-intensive courses several times a year. Enrolment covers unlimited access to a multimedia lab with audio and video cassettes, DVDs, TV, books and magazines. ◈ *Centro Linguistico Interfacoltà, Ramo dell'Agnello, S Croce 2161* • *Map L1* • *041 234 9711* • *www.unive.it/cli*

3 Istituto Venezia Italian Language Courses
Group and individual courses in Italian language and culture are held year-round at the institute, and the school can also arrange family or private accommodation for students. ◈ *Campo Santa Margherita, Dorsoduro 3116/a* • *Map K5* • *041 522 4331* • *www.istituto venezia.com*

4 Watercolour Painting
Spend an intensive week in the open air on a summer watercolour course, or drawing, fresco painting, self-portraiture and printmaking. The internationally known school can accommodate students in its apartments. ◈ *Scuola Internazionale di Grafica, Calle del Cristo Cannaregio 1798* • *Map C1* • *041 721 950* • *www.scuolagrafica.it*

5 Restoration Techniques
The Venice European Centre for the Trades and Professions of the Conservation of Architectural Heritage on the island of San Servolo (see p116) runs courses in restoration of everything from stone and stucco work to wrought iron and mosaics. ◈ *Isola di S Servolo* • *Map H1* • *041 526 8546* • *www.centroeuropeo mestieri.com*

6 Glassmaking
Expert craftsmen run courses not only in glassblowing and beads, but also stucco, furniture restoration and artistic glass. ◈ *Confartigianato, Calle Carminati, Castello 5653/4* • *041 529 9270* • *www.artigianivenezia.it*

7 Ceramics
Small groups are instructed by Sybille Heller in the art of hand-moulded, wheel-turned pottery and a variety of decorative techniques. Courses commence in March and September, and are held two afternoons a week. ◈ *La Ciotola, Via Candia 24, Lido (near Palazzo del Cinema)* • *Map H2* • *041 242 0308* • *www. venezialaciotola.com*

8 Italian Cooking
Qualified chef Fulvia starts her short-term and year-round cooking courses with a visit to the Rialto market (see p28) to familiarize food buffs with the ingredients they will be practising on in her marvellous home. ◈ *Fulvia Sesani, Ramo del Pestrin, Castello 6140* • *Map F3* • *041 522 8923* • *fulvia.sesani@ bitcomputer.it*

9 Mask-making
Starting with the clay mould, you learn to produce and decorate a papier-mâché mask at the short courses held in the Ca' Macana workshop. For people who don't mind getting their hands dirty. Courses are taught in various European languages. ◈ *Calle delle Botteghe, Dorsoduro 3172* • *Map K6* • *041 277 6142* • *www.camacana.com*

10 Rowing
Enrol for traditional standing-up style Veneto rowing lessons at this prestigious club. Courses are usually held in spring, though retirees are often on hand to help beginners at other times. ◈ *Canottieri Bucintoro Zattere, Dorsoduro 15* • *Map D5* • *041 520 5630*

Left **Cipriani garden** Right **Excelsior**

Luxury Hotels

1 Cipriani

Set on its own glorious island, the famed Cipriani is a matter of minutes across the water by exclusive launch to Piazza San Marco. It has a private garden with a salt-water pool, and three top-class restaurants *(see p58)*. ⌨ *Giudecca 10 • Map E6 • 041 520 7744 • www. hotelcipriani.it • Closed Jan–Feb • €€€€€*

2 Luna Hotel Baglioni

Exquisite service in a sophisticated atmosphere of chandeliers and marble. This is Venice's oldest hotel and hosted Templar knights in the 1100s waiting to embark for the Crusades. Breakfast is served in the drawing room frescoed by pupils of Tiepolo *(see p44)*. ⌨ *Calle Larga dell' Ascension, S Marco 1243 • Map P5 • 041 528 9840 • www.baglionihotels.com • €€€€€*

3 Gritti Palace

Hemingway stayed in this 15th-century palace-hotel located on the Grand Canal. Romantic waterside dining is among the features. ⌨ *Campo S Maria del Giglio, S Marco 2467 • Map N6 • 041 794 611 • www.luxurycollection.com/ grittipalace • €€€€€*

4 Hotel Danieli

While the service leaves much to be desired, the hotel's history *(see p101)* attracts many guests. The best rooms are in the old wing, overlooking the Riva degli Schiavoni. ⌨ *Riva degli Schiavoni, Castello 4196 • Map R5 • 041 522 6480 • www.starwoodhotels. com • €€€€€*

5 Hotel Des Bains

This luxurious and discreet Lido hotel has its own swimming pool, tennis courts and private beach area. It also served as the backdrop for Visconti's film *Death in Venice (see p67)*. ⌨ *Lungomare Marconi 17, Lido • Map H2 • 041 526 5921 • www.westin.com • Closed Nov–mid-Mar • No disabled access • €€€€€*

6 Grand Hotel Palazzo dei Dogi

With a marvellous garden stretching back to the lagoon, this former convent on a quiet Cannaregio canal is superbly furnished with Murano chandeliers and fabrics crafted by leading artisans. Best value luxury hotel in town with its own guest launch. ⌨ *Fondamenta Madonna dell'Orto, Cannaregio 3500 • Map D1 • 041 220 8111 • www.boscolo hotels.com • €€€€€*

7 Excelsior Palace

Crawling with stars and paparazzi during the summer Film Festival *(see p62)*, this graceful mega-hotel has magnificent rooms right on the beach. A swimming pool and exclusive restaurants are also a feature. ⌨ *Lungomare Marconi 41, Lido • Map H2 • 041 526 0201 • www.westin.com • Closed Nov–mid-Mar • €€€€€*

8 Metropole

Majestic good value establishment, immaculately run. On the waterfront only minutes from San Marco, it boasts a wonderful garden, a perfect antidote from the city streets. ⌨ *Riva degli Schiavoni, Castello 4149 • Map F4 • 041 520 5044 • www.hotelmetropole.com • €€€€*

9 Europa & Regina

Sumptuous decor in this elegant historic palace right on the Grand Canal, close to the Piazza San Marco. ⌨ *Corte Barozzi, S Marco 2159 • Map P6 • 041 520 0477 • www.westin.com • No disabled access • €€€€€*

10 Ca' Pisani

A warm ambience, stunning modern design, steam bath and all the facilities you could hope for. You'll never want to leave this 15th-century palace near Accademia, converted in 2000. ⌨ *Rio Terrà Foscarini, Dorsoduro 979/a • Map F4 • 041 240 1411 • www.capisanihotel.it • No disabled access • €€€–€€€€*

 Note: *Unless otherwise stated, all hotels accept credit cards, have en-suite bathrooms and air conditioning*

Left **Casa Cardinal Piazza** Right **Hotel Gobbo sign**

🔟 Budget Hotels

1 Casa Cardinal Piazza

Great-value palace guesthouse run by friendly nuns and set in a shady garden right on the lagoon edge. Breakfast available; 11pm curfew.
⊗ *Fondamenta Contarini, Cannaregio 3539/A • Map D1 • 041 721 388 • No credit cards • No Air-conditioning • No disabled access • €*

2 Archie's House

The cheapest backpacker's option in town, close to the San Leonardo market with heaps of cafés and trattorias, and only 10 minutes from the station. Just turn up for a bed and you'll be greeted by an eccentric Chinese-Italian family. Rates get lower depending on the number of occupants for a room and length of stay. Internet. ⊗ *Rio Terrà S Leonardo, Cannaregio 1814/B • Map C2 • 041 720 884 • reception closes 1–5pm • No credit cards • No disabled access • €*

3 Alloggi Gerotto Calderan

Handy for the station, with airy rooms, some with bath (no breakfast). Clientele are welcomed by enthusiastic English-speaking staff. Bargain down the rates in low season. ⊗ *Campo S Geremia, Cannaregio 283 • Map C2 • 041 715 361 • www.casagerottocalderan. com • No credit cards • No disabled access • €*

4 Il Lato Azzurro

Great-value lodgings on this garden island where sea breezes are ensured. They arrange canoe trips, bicycles, picnic lunches and half board, entailing mainly vegetarian meals with locally grown produce. ⊗ *Via Forti 13, Sant'Erasmo • Map H2 • 041 523 0642 • www.latoazzurro.it • No air conditioning • €*

5 Istituto Artigianelli

Close to the sunny Zattere, this religious-trade institution has new modern rooms with bath. Book in advance.
⊗ *Rio Terrà Foscarini, Dorsoduro 909/A • Map C5 • 041 522 4077 • www.donorione-venezia.it • €€*

6 Domus Civica

These university rooms are available in the summer months (Jul–Sep). Discounts for students and Rolling Venice participants (see p137). No meals, but plenty of cafés in the vicinity.
⊗ *Campiello Chiovere, S Polo 3082 • Map B3 • 041 721 103 • No en suite bathrooms • No air conditioning • No disabled access • www.domuscivica. com • €*

7 Al Gobbo

The "Hunchback" is a clean small-scale hotel with a couple of rooms overlooking a bustling square. Easy access from the railway station.
⊗ *Campo S Geremia 312, Cannaregio • Map C2 • 041 715 001 • www. albergoalgobbo.it • No air conditioning • No disabled access • €*

8 Al Campaniel Guesthouse

Spanish-Venetian couple Gloria and Marco are discreet and highly professional hosts who offer spotless rooms close to the San Tomà boat stop. Each room has tea- and coffee-making facilities.
⊗ *Calle del Campanile, S Polo 2889 • Map L4 • 041 275 07 49 • www.al campaniel.com • No disabled access • €*

9 Istituto Canossiano

A modernized, converted convent with vast courtyards to wander around. Automatic distributing machines for snacks and drinks, otherwise it's not far to the Zattere. There's a midnight curfew.
⊗ *Fondamenta delle Eremite, Dorsoduro 1323 • Map K6 • 041 240 97 13 • cvenezia@fdcc.org • No air conditioning • No disabled access • €*

10 Al Santo

This simple hotel is very conveniently located, only a 10-minute stroll from Padua's main sights (see p123).
⊗ *Via del Santo 147, Padua • 049 875 2131 • www.alsanto.it • €–€€*

Left **Locanda Cipriani** Right **Hotel Marconi**

TOP 10 Hotels with Charm

1 Pensione La Calcina

In 1877 Ruskin stayed at this guesthouse on the Zattere, as the friendly staff eagerly explain. Of course, the rooms have been modernized since those days but they have retained their charm and parquet floors. An exclusive street-level terrace overlooks the Giudecca Canal, while another surveys the rooftops. Advance reservations are essential. Ⓢ *Zattere, Dorsoduro 780 • Map D5 • 041 520 6466 • www.lacalcina.com • No disabled access • €€€*

Pensione La Calcina

2 Accademia Villa Maravege

Book well ahead to stay in this beautiful 17th-century villa near the Accademia *(see pp24–5)*, which was formerly the Russian embassy. Breakfast can be enjoyed in the private garden. Ⓢ *Fondamenta Bollani, Dorsoduro 1058 • Map L6 • 041 521 0188 • www. pensioneaccademia.it • No disabled access • €€€*

3 Giorgione

A comfortable 4-star hotel with high standards, a warm reception and a pretty garden. Last-minute special offers. Ⓢ *Calle Larga dei Proverbi, Cannaregio 4587 • Map E3 • 041 522 5810 • www. hotelgiorgione.com • €€€*

4 Ca' della Corte

Charming bed-and-breakfast with spotless rooms, which boast all the latest equipment, such as satellite TV. Very handy to Piazzale Roma. Ⓢ *Corte Surian, Dorsoduro 3560 • Map B3 • 041 715 877 • www.cadellacorte. com • No disabled access • €–€€€*

5 Hotel Flora

Though small, the pretty courtyard with creeping greenery is an oasis of calm after the city crowds. Good views from the upper rooms. Ⓢ *Calle Bergamaschi, S Marco 2283/A • Map P5 • 041 520 5844 • www.hotelflora.it • No disabled access • €€€*

6 Locanda Cipriani

A peaceful, sophisticated place on the island of Torcello *(see pp30–31)*, with a list of illustrious past guests. A famed restaurant overlooks a garden, and you are allowed to explore the island after the day-trippers have left. Ⓢ *Piazza S Fosca 29, Torcello • Map H1 • 041 730 150*

• www.locandacipriani.com • No disabled access • Closed Jan • €€€

7 Ca' del Borgo

Charming 15th-century villa located on the southern end of the Lido, in an old fishing village. Easy access to Venice and the beach. Ⓢ *Piazza delle Erbe 8, Malamocco • Map F1 • 041 770 749 • www. cadelborgo.com • €€€*

8 Hotel Marconi

Popular hotel by Rialto Bridge, with outside seating reserved for guests. Warm reception though simple rooms. Ⓢ *Riva del Vin, S Polo 729 • Map P3 • 041 522 2068 • www.hotelmarconi.it • No disabled access • €€–€€€€*

9 San Simon Ai Due Fanali

Tastefully renovated former monastery – rooms feature wooden rafters. Several apartments are available. Ⓢ *Campo S Simeone Grande, S Croce 946/949 • Map K1 • 041 718 490 • www.aiduefanali.com • No disabled access • €€*

10 Villa Giustinian

An 18th-century villa with a swimming pool, park, magnificent rooms and a fine restaurant. A 40-minute bus trip to Venice. Buses pass every 20 minutes. Ⓢ *Via Miranese 85, Mirano • 041 570 0200 • www. villagiustinian.com • €€*

  Note: *Unless otherwise stated, all hotels accept credit cards, have en-suite bathrooms and air conditioning*

Left **Locanda San Barnaba** Right **Tourist luggage**

🔟 Converted Palaces

1 Hotel San Stefano
Discerning style, maximum comfort (Jacuzzi in all rooms) and breathtaking views. Great care is taken with details in this slender tall palace. ◈ *Campo S Stefano, S Marco 2957 • Map M5 • 041 520 0166 • www.hotelsantostefanovenezia.com • No disabled access • €€€€*

2 San Cassiano – Ca' Favretto
Right on the Grand Canal, but hidden away in the maze of alleyways close to Rialto, is a 10th-century palace, converted into a hotel named after a 19th-century artist. Elegant rooms with all mod cons. ◈ *Calle della Rosa, S Croce 2232 • Map N2 • 041 524 1768 • www.sancassiano.it • No disabled access • €€€–€€€€*

3 Locanda San Barnaba
Minutes from the Ca' Rezzonico ferry stop, a quiet, elegant palazzo hotel, with original frescoes in many of the rooms, which are named after Goldoni's plays. ◈ *Calle del Traghetto, Dorsoduro 2785–2786 • Map L5 • 041 241 1233 • www.locanda-sanbarnaba.com • No disabled access • €€–€€€*

4 La Residenza
In a pretty square behind the Riva degli Schiavoni *(see p101)*, a rather ramshackle but authentic palace atmosphere greets guests. The rooms are modest but comfortable. ◈ *Campo Bandiera e Moro, Castello 3608 • Map F4 • 041 528 5315 • www.venicelaresidenza.com • No disabled access • €€*

5 Casa Verardo
Beautifully renovated small-scale palace featuring an atmospheric salon with antique furniture where breakfast is served. A pretty terrace overlooks a canal. Internet access and full bar service. ◈ *Ponte Storto, 4765 Castello • Map F3 • 041 528 6138 • www.casaverardo.it • €€–€€€*

6 Locanda Leon Bianco
Parquet floors alternate with Venetian terrazzo in this modest atmospheric palazzo, in a quiet backwater just over the bridge from Campo SS Apostoli. A couple of rooms look across the Grand Canal to Rialto. ◈ *Corte del Leon Bianco, Cannaregio 5629 • Map P2 • 041 523 3572 • www.leonbianco.it • No disabled access • €€*

7 Albergo Guerrato
Charming old place at Rialto, saturated with history and dating back to 1288. No great views but heaps of charm and space. ◈ *Calle drio la Scimia, S Polo 240/a • Map N2 • 041 522 7131 • www.pensioneguerrato.it • Not all rooms have en-suite bath • No disabled access • €€*

8 Locanda La Corte
A relaxing atmosphere prevails in this renovated 16th-century palace. It once served the ambassador from Brescia and is impeccably furnished with period pieces. Breakfast is served in the courtyard. ◈ *Calle Bressana, Castello 6317 • Map F3 • 041 241 1300 • www.locandalacorte.it • No disabled access • €–€€€*

9 Villa Ducale
Halfway between Padua and Venice, this stately residence stands in a lovely private park with statues, while the beautiful rooms have all mod cons plus frescoes and glass chandeliers. ◈ *Riviera Martiri della Libertà 75, Dolo • ACTV bus (53) from Piazzale Roma • 041 560 8020 • www.villaducale.it • No disabled access • €€–€€€*

10 Al Sole
A beautiful place to stay, convenient for Piazzale Roma, this 16th-century palace is often used as a film set, with a huge lobby and a courtyard draped in wisteria. Rooms have all mod cons. ◈ *Fondamenta Minotto, S Croce 136 • Map J4 • 041 710 844 • www.alsolehotels.com • €€€*

Left **Dell'Alboro** Right **Locanda Fiorita**

⑩ Hotels in Tranquil Locations

Streetsmart

1 Hotel Falier
This cheery place is named after the beheaded traitor Doge Falier, "as a warning to guests who fail to pay!" Sunlight streams into the comfortable if small rooms, all of them come complete with shower, and there's a courtyard dripping with wisteria.
Ⓢ *Salizzada S Pantalon, S Croce 130 • Map K4 • 041 710 882 • www.hotelfalier.com • No disabled access • €€€*

2 Locanda ai Bareteri
Sergio and Laura are the hosts in this bed-and-breakfast, sandwiched between the Mercerie shopping thoroughfare and a quieter alley. Highlights are old *trompe l'oeil* stained glass, terrazzo flooring and internet facilities.
Ⓢ *Calle di Mezzo, S Marco 4966 • Map Q4 • 041 523 2233 • www.bareteri.com • No disabled access • €€€*

3 Locanda Fiorita
A very pretty place on a sunny square which was once a public cemetery, off Campo San Stefano. In spring and summer you can enjoy a leisurely breakfast outside. Bargain for cheaper rooms in low season.
Ⓢ *Campiello Novo o dei Morti, S Marco 3457/A • Map M5 • 041 523 4754 • www.locandafiorita.com • No disabled access • €€*

4 Canada
Fairly ordinary but excellently placed, despite the never-ending stairs. A matter of minutes on foot to both Piazza San Marco or Rialto. Several rooms boast canal views, while others have their own roof terrace.
Ⓢ *Campo S Lio, Castello 5659 • Map Q3 • 041 522 9912 • www.canadavenice.com • No disabled access • €€€*

5 Ca' San Marcuola
In a handy location close to the vaporetto stop, this unpretentious but quiet and friendly guesthouse has all mod cons. Ⓢ *Campiello della Chiesa, Cannaregio 1763 • Map C2 • 041 716 048 • www.casanmarcuola.com • No disabled access • €€*

6 Hotel Villa Rosa
Apart from one special room with its own verandah, most rooms rate average in terms of comfort here. However the location is excellent, in a quiet alley close to the railway station.
Ⓢ *Calle Misericordia, Cannaregio 389 • Map B2 • 041 718 976 • www.villarosahotel.com • €€*

7 Due Mori
In a quiet traffic-free street in Vicenza, close to all the main sights *(see p124)*, the Due Mori has spacious spotless rooms furnished in old-style dark timber.

Ⓢ *Contrà Do Rode 26, Vicenza (pedestrian zone, 10 mins from station) • 044 432 1886 • www.hotelduemori.com • No air conditioning • €*

8 San Giorgio Monastery
The monks on San Giorgio island welcome guests to their peaceful premises. A simple breakfast is provided and self-catering is available.
Ⓢ *Isola di San Giorgio Maggiore • Map F5 • 041 241 4717; fax 041 520 6579 • No credit cards • €*

9 Hotel Canaletto
The great artist Canaletto *(see p44)* lived in this quiet square, only minutes from both the Piazza San Marco and Rialto. Elegant period decor, all mod cons, and several rooms with canal views. Ⓢ *Calle della Malvasia, Castello 5487 • Map Q3 • 041 522 0518 • www.hotelcanaletto.com • No disabled access • €€€*

10 Dell'Alboro
Located in a relaxing residential area near the Sant'Angelo boat stop, this rather plain hotel nevertheless has rooms with all modern facilities and is very central for Piazza San Marco.
Ⓢ *Corte dell'Alboro, S Marco 3894/A-B • Map M4 • 041 522 9454 • www.alborohotel.it • No disabled access • €€€–€€€€*

Note: *Unless otherwise stated, all hotels accept credit cards, have en suite bathrooms and air conditioning*

Left **Room in Al Gazzettino** Right **Bel Sito & Berlino**

🔟 Medium-Priced Hotels

1 Rossi
Recommended family hotel, high on hospitality. Spotless rooms, many with lovely views, and conveniently placed for Strada Nova. Book well in advance.
🔦 *Calle Procuratie, Cannaregio 262 • Map C2 • 041 715 164 • www. hotelrossi.ve.it • No disabled access • €*

2 Locanda Ca' Zose
Cosy immaculate rooms, several with enchanting canal views, run by sisters Graziella and Valentina. Very quiet, handy for La Salute vaporetto and the Guggenheim.
🔦 *Calle del Bastion, Dorsoduro 193/B • Map D5 • 041 522 6635 • www. hotelcazose.com • No disabled access • €€–€€€*

3 Hotel alla Salute Da Cici
Ezra Pound spent time in this hotel set in the Salute residential area, a stone's throw from the Zattere, not to mention Accademia (see pp24–5) and Guggenheim galleries (see pp24–5).
🔦 *Fondamenta Ca' Balà, Dorsoduro 222 • 041 523 5404 • Map D5 • www. hotelsalute.com • No disabled access • €€*

4 Bel Sito & Berlino
A well-placed 3-star hotel facing the Baroque wonders of the Chiesa di Santa Maria del Giglio (see p38). The decor is old style and the atmosphere is warm.
🔦 *Campo S Maria del Giglio, S Marco 2517 • Map N6 • 041 522 3365 • www.hotelbelsito.info • €€–€€€*

5 Al Gazzettino
Centrally located between Rialto and San Marco, this is a basic, decent value hotel. The downstairs walls are papered with sheets from the city's *Il Gazzettino* newspaper, a long-standing neighbour until its relocation to the more practical mainland.
🔦 *Calle di Mezzo, S Marco 4971 • Map Q4 • 041 528 6523 • www.algazzettino. com • No disabled access • €€*

6 Hotel Fontana
Family-managed 2-star establishment in a quiet spot just around the corner from San Zaccaria. Very much a middle-of-the-road place with kitschy decor but satellite TV.
🔦 *Campo S Provolo, Castello 4701 • Map F4 • 041 522 0579 • www.hotelfontana.it • No disabled access • €€€*

7 Al Gambero
A guaranteed old favourite on a bridge halfway between Rialto and the Piazza San Marco, wonderful for many sights and shopping sprees. Downstairs is Le Bistrot, a popular nightspot (see p61).
🔦 *Calle dei Fabbri, S Marco 4687 • Map P4 • 041 522 4384 • www.locandaal gambero.com • No disabled access • €€€*

8 Locanda SS Giovanni e Paolo
Breakfast is served in this handy guesthouse, only 5 mins from Piazza San Marco. 🔦 *Barbaria de le Tole, Castello 6401 • Map R2 • 041 522 2767 • www. locandassgiovannipaolo.it • No disabled access • €–€€*

9 Locanda Sant'Anna
Despite its dingy appearance and impossible to find location, this guesthouse in down-to-earth Castello is friendly and popular, particularly during the Biennale art exhibitions held every two years (see p62).
🔦 *Corte Bianco, Castello 269 • Map F3 • 041 528 6466 • www.locanda santanna.com • No disabled access • €–€€*

10 Hotel Torcolo
You could hardly wish for a more central location in Verona, just around the corner from the Arena. Nothing exceptional, but friendly and clean. Guest parking available.
🔦 *Vicolo Listone 3, Verona • Bus nos. 11, 12, 13 (or 91, 92 evenings & hols) • 045 800 7512 • www.hotel torcolo.it • No disabled access • €*

Left **Venetian apartment balcony view** Centre & right **Venetian apartment interiors**

10 Self-Catering

1 Venetian Apartments

This UK company rents out studios, family-size apartments with terraces through to wonderful *piano nobile* floors of luxury palazzos *(see p43)* on the Grand Canal. They also provide plenty of helpful information on practical matters. ◈ *403 Parkway House, Sheen Lane, London SW14 8LS, UK* • *020 8878 1130* • *www.venice-rentals.com* • *€€–€€€€€*

2 Veronica Tomasso Cotgrove

Another UK company offers short- or long-term rentals, with a choice of 30 apartments to sleep from two to seven people, and even the chance of a garden, a rarity for Venice. Costs vary depending on location and facilities. ◈ *10 St Palazzos Crescent, London NW1 7TS, UK* • *020 7267 2423* • *www.vtcitaly.com* • *€€€€€*

3 Carefree Italy

Of their 20 properties available for holiday rents, this UK company includes a lovely apartment in Cannaregio complete with rooftop views. They also arrange for rental of private villas in the Veneto area. ◈ *Zurich House, East Park, Crawley, W Sussex RH10 6AJ* • *01293 552277* • *www.carefree-italy.com* • *€€–€€€€€*

4 Belvedere Italia

A select range of prime properties owned by long-standing families, including an atmospheric home near Accademia. ◈ *74a St John's Wood High St, London NW8 7SH* • *020 758 64164* • *www.belvedere-italia.com* • *€€€€€*

5 Sant'Angelo Immobiliare

Long-established Venice estate agent with 20 fully equipped houses to rent by the week. Several have roof terraces and weekend stays are possible. Services such as cell phone rental and cleaning included. ◈ *Campo Sant'Angelo, S Marco 3818* • *Map N5* • *041 522 1505* • *www.venicehouse.it* • *€–€€€€€*

6 Mitwohnzentrale Venice Alternative Accommodation

Venetian resident Helga Gross is in an excellent position to advise on the 150 fully furnished properties she deals with and will rent you a room or a palace from five nights to up to a year. ◈ *Calle S Antonio, Castello 5448A* • *Map H5* • *041 523 16 72* • *www.mwz-online.com* • *€–€€€€€*

7 MyItalianVacation

An efficient US company that manages a vast spectrum of 34 modest and luxurious apartments in Venice with room for up to seven occupants. All are personally inspected. ◈ *3622 49th Ave SW, Seattle, WA 98116, USA* • *888 465 1460* • *www.myItalianVacation. com* • *€€€–€€€€€*

8 Venice Real Estate

The very top in prestigious apartments and luxury residences in Venice proper are available. Most have a fantastic panoramic roof terrace. ◈ *Calle Tron, S Marco 1130* • *Map Q4* • *041 521 0622* • *www.venicerealestate.it* • *€€€–€€€€€*

9 Rentavilla

In operation since 1983, US-based Villanet has 29 places to rent in Venice, some large enough for up to seven people. They can also arrange for car and phone rental. ◈ *1251 NW 116th St, Seattle, WA 98177, USA* • *800 964 1891* • *www.rentavilla.com* • *€–€€€€€*

10 Vacanza Bella

Fifteen prestigious holiday homes are available in Venice itself, most with all mod cons included as well as scenic balconies. Help in the form of cleaning and other services can also be arranged. ◈ *2261 Market St, PMB 281 San Francisco, CA 94114, USA* • *415 554 0234* • *www. vbella.com* • *€€€–€€€€€*

 Note: *Although prices are quoted on a nightly rate most apartments will be hired out weekly*

Price Categories

Prices per night (with breakfast if included), taxes and extra charges.	€ under €100
	€€ €100–€150
	€€€ €150–€250
	€€€€ €250–€350
	€€€€€ over €350

Left **IYH Ostello Venezia** Right **Ostello Santa Fosca**

🔟 Hostels and Camp Sites

1 IYH Ostello Venezia

Well-run hostel offering cheap meals and a beautiful setting on Giudecca, a 35-minute *vaporetto* trip from the railway station (line No. 82) and five minutes to Piazza San Marco *(see pp16–19)*. ⬡ Fondamenta Zitelle 86, Giudecca • Map E6 • 041 523 8211 • www. ostellionline.org • €

2 Ostello Santa Fosca

University student hostel which lets out dorm beds to backpackers in, rambling convent grounds. Cooking facilities are available in summer. ⬡ Fondamenta Canal Diedo, Cannaregio 2372 • Map D2 • 041 715 733 • www.santafosca.it • €

3 Foresteria Valdese

A wonderful place to stay near Campo Santa Maria Formosa *(see p102)*, Palazzo Cavagnis is a guesthouse run by the Waldensian and Methodist community and has frescoed dormitories, nice rooms and apartments for families. Advance booking essential. ⬡ Calle Lunga S Maria Formosa, Castello 51/0 • Map R3 • 041 528 6797 • www. diaconiavaldese.org/venezia • €

4 Campeggio Miramare

One of the many camping grounds at Punta Sabbioni on the sea-side of Venice. Linked to the city by ferry (line LN). Huts and camp sites. ⬡ 041 966 150 • Open Apr–Nov • www.camping-miramare.it

5 Camping Fusina

Popular three-star venue for campers and backpackers (in a caravan), right on the lagoon edge. Well connected by bus No. 11 from Mestre railway station or the Alilaguna ferry from the Zattere in Venice. Open year-round. ⬡ Via Moranzani 79, Fusina • 041 547 0055 • www.camping-fusina.com • €

6 Camping Alba d'Oro

Only 2 km (1 mile) from the airport (bus No. 15), this spacious camp site has a swimming pool, internet point, pizzeria and shops. Tent-less visitors sleep in cabins. Closed December to February. ⬡ Via Triestina 214/b, Tessera • Map G1 • 041 541 5102 • www.ecvacanze.it • €

7 IYH Ostello di Mira

This recently opened hostel is located just outside Venice in a lovely country setting. Car parking is available. All linen is provided. Closed October to February. ⬡ Via Giare 169, Giare di Mira • Venice-Chioggia bus line, Giare stop • 041 567 9203 • www.casasoleluna.it • €

8 IYH Città di Padova

A bit out of the way, but it is only a short walk to the main sights. The hostel also benefits from a surprisingly beautiful setting in an ornamental grassy square. ⬡ Via Aleardo Aleardi 30, Padova • Bus Nos. 3, 8, 12, 18 or 22 from Padua railway station to Prato della Valle • 049 875 2219 • www. ostellopadova.it • €

9 IYH Ostello Olimpico

A cheery, helpful hostel close to both the town's main Tourist Office and the Teatro Olimpico *(see p123)*. Meals available at a special low price at a neighbouring bar and restaurant. Internet point and bike hire available. Closed one month in winter. ⬡ Viale Giuriolo 7, Vicenza • Bus Nos. 1, 2, 5 or 7 from the railway station • 044 454 0222 • www.ostellionline.org • €

10 IYH Ostello Villa Francescatti

This beautiful 16th-century villa on the hillside above the Roman amphitheatre doubles as the official youth hostel, with dormitory accommodation. It is only 3 km (2 miles) from Verona's railway station. Evening meals are available. ⬡ Salita Fontana del Ferro 15, Verona • Bus No. 73 (Mon–Sat), 90 (evenings & Sun) from the railway station • 045 590 360 • €

 Note: Price categories for hostels and camp sites are per person per night and range between €6–30

General Index

Index

Acknowledgements

The Author
Gillian Price was born in England in 1953 but grew up in Sydney, Australia. She moved to Venice in 1981 and has written nine books on walking in Italy. Gillian has been contributing to Dorling Kindersley's Eyewitness Travel Guides since 1998.

Produced by Book Creation Services Ltd, London

Project Editor Zoë Ross
Art Editor Alison Verity
Designer Ann Fisher
Picture Research Monica Allende
Proofreader Stewart J Wild
Indexer Hilary Bird
Design and Editorial Assistance Tamiko Rex, Laura de Selincourt, Jo Ann Titmarsh, Beatriz Waller

Main Photographer Demetrio Carasco

Additional Photography John Heseltine, Gillian Price, Roger Moss

Illustrator Chris Orr & Associates

Cartography Pam Alford, James Anderson, Jane Voss (Anderson Geographics Ltd)

FOR DORLING KINDERSLEY:
Editor Karen Villabona
Senior Editor Marcus Hardy
Senior Art Editor Marisa Renzullo
Cartography Co-ordinator Casper Morris
Senior DTP Designer Jason Little
Production Sarah Dodd, Marie Ingledew
Publishing Manager Kate Poole
Senior Publishing Manager Louise Bostock Lang
Director of Publishing Gillian Allan

Special Assistance Carlo Alberto Albrigo, Tamara Andruszkiewicz, Bruce Boreham, Gianni Cadel, Martin Price, Nicola Regine, Laura Sabbadin, Sally Spector, Venice, Padua, Vicenza and Verona tourist offices, Venice Hoteliers' Association.

Picture Credits
t-top; tc-top centre; tr-top right; cla-centre left above; ca-centre above; cra-centre right above; cl-centre left; c-centre; cr-centre right; clb-centre left below; cb-centre below; crb-centre right below; bl-below left; bc-below centre; br-below right.

The publishers would like to thank the following individuals, companies and picture libraries for permission to reproduce their photographs:

AISA,Barcelona: 11b, 20–21c, 52tl, 86-87, 106-10;. AKG, London: 31br,34t, 35b, 50tl, 50tcr, 50tr 50b, © ADAGP, Paris and DACS, London 2001 "The Bird in Space" 1925 by Brancusi 7t, © Succession Picasso/DACS London 2001 "The Poet" by Picasso 34b, ©ADAGP, Paris and DACS, London 2001 "Dressing the Bride" by Max Ernst 34-35c, "Portrait of Vivaldi" by Morellon 52b; Cameraphoto: 11t, 45tl, 45tr, "The Victorious Return of Doge Andrea Contarini after the Triumph in Chioggia" (detail) Paolo Veronese 15b, "Triumph of Venetia as Queen of the Seas" Tintoretto 14b, "Bathing Venus" by Antonio Canova 18b, "Supper in the House of Levi" by Veronese 24-25c, "Portrait" by Rosalba Carriera 25cr, "Mary with Child" by Bellini 44tc, "Portrait of Caterina Conaro" 53b; St Domingie-M. Rabatti: "La Tempesta" by Giorgione 24t; Erich Lessing: 44tl, "Piere di Cadore" by Titian 44tr, "Rio dei Medicanti" by Canaletto 44b; AL GAZZETINO: 149tl; ALLSPORT: 62b; © DACS London 2001 "The Magic Garden" by Paul Klee 35cr; BAROVIER & TOSO, Murano:112tl; BISTRO DE VENISE: 60tl; BRIDGEMAN ART LIBRARY: San Giobbe Altarpiece c.1487 by Bellini 7bl, 24b, © ADAGP, Paris and DACS, London 2001 "Studio with a Fruit Bowl" by Dufy 41c; CAPELLINA PALLADIO: 128tl; CORBIS: 4-5, 19b, 20-21, 21b, 66b, 70-71, 120-121, 126tr, 130-13; IUAV Istituto Universitario di Architetture di Venezia: 55; MARY EVANS PICTURE LIBRARY: 50tcl, 51t, 52c, 52tr; LOCANDA FIORITA: 149tr; ESTHER LABI: 128tl; HOTEL MARIN: 149tr; MARKA: 62tc, M.Albonico 62tr, Barbazza 115b, 132tc, M.Cristofoti 122tl, D.Donadoni 123b, 126tl, 127tr, E.Lasagni 129tl, M. Mazzola 127tr, M.Silvano 123 tr, G.Luigi Sosso 144tr; MERCADO D'ORIENTE: 128tr; NARDI: 68tr; NEWIMAGE: David Bardi 141tr; Rolando Fabriani 28bl; Nicola Quaranti 140tr; TEATRO FONDAMENTA NUOVE: Giovanni Pancino 67cl; TOURISM VENEZIA: La Fotografica 137tc; VENETIAN APARTMENTS: all top

All other images are © DK. For further information see www.dkimages.com.

Special Editions of DK Travel Guides

DK Travel Guides can be purchased in bulk quantities at discounted prices for use in promotions or as premiums. We are also able to offer special editions and personalized jackets, corporate imprints, and excerpts from all of our books, tailored specifically to meet your own needs.

To find out more, please contact:

(in the United States) **SpecialSales@dk.com**

(in the UK) **Sarah.Burgess@dk.com**

(in Canada) DK Special Sales at **general@tourmaline.ca**

(in Australia) **business.development@pearson.com.au**

Phrase Book

In an Emergency

Help!	**Aiuto!**	eye-yoo-toh
Stop!	**Fermate!**	fair-mah-teh
Call a doctor.	**Chiama un medico**	kee-ah-mah oon meh-dee-koh
Call an ambulance.	**Chiama un' ambulanza**	kee-ah-mah oon am-boo-lan-tsa
Call the police.	**Chiama la polizia**	kee-ah-mah lah pol-ee-tsee-ah
Call the fire brigade.	**Chiama i pompieri**	kee-ah-mah ee pom-pee-air-ee

Communication Essentials

Yes/No	**Sì/No**	see/noh
Please	**Per favore**	pair fah-vor-eh
Thank you	**Grazie**	grah-tsee-eh
Excuse me	**Mi scusi**	mee skoo-zee
Hello	**Buon giorno**	bwon jor-noh
Goodbye	**Arrivederci**	ah-ree-veh-dair-chee
Good evening	**Buona sera**	bwon-ah sair-ah
What?	**Quale?**	kwah-leh?
When?	**Quando?**	kwan-doh?
Why?	**Perchè?**	pair-keh?
Where?	**Dove?**	doh-veh?

Useful Phrases

How are you?	**Come sta?**	koh-meh stah?
Very well, thank you.	**Molto bene, grazie.**	moll-toh beh-neh grah-tsee-eh
Pleased to meet you.	**Piacere di conoscerla.**	pee-ah-chair-eh dee-coh-noh-shair-lah
That's fine.	**Va bene.**	va beh-neh
Where is/are ...?	**Dov'è? Dove sono ...?**	dov-eh/doveh soh-noh?
How do I get to ...?	**Come faccio per arrivare a ...?**	koh-meh fah choh pair arri-var-eh ah..?
Do you speak English?	**Parla inglese?**	par-lah een-gleh-zeh?
I don't understand.	**Non capisco.**	non ka-pee-skoh
I'm sorry.	**Mi dispiace.**	mee dee-spee-ah-cheh

Shopping

How much does this cost?	**Quant'è, per favore?**	kwan-teh pair fah-vor-eh?
I would like ...	**Vorrei ...**	vor-ray
Do you have ...?	**Avete ...?**	ah-veh-teh.. ?
Do you take credit cards?	**Accettate carte di credito?**	ah-chet-tah-teh kar-teh dee creh-dee-toh?
What time do you open/close?	**A che ora apre/ chiude?**	ah keh or-ah ah-preh/kee-oo-deh?
this one	**questo**	kweh-stoh
that one	**quello**	kwell-oh
expensive	**caro**	kar-oh
cheap	**a buon prezzo**	ah bwon pret-soh
size, clothes	**la taglia**	lah tah-lee-ah
size, shoes	**il numero**	eel noo-mair-oh
white	**bianco**	bee-ang-koh
black	**nero**	neh-roh
red	**rosso**	ross-oh
yellow	**giallo**	jal-loh
green	**verde**	vair-deh
blue	**blu**	bloo

Types of Shop

bakery	**il forno /il panificio**	eel forn-oh /eel pan-ee-fee-choh
bank	**la banca**	lah bang-kah
bookshop	**la libreria**	lah lee-breh-ree-ah
cake shop	**la pasticceria**	lah pas-tee-chair-ee-ah
chemist	**la farmacia**	lah far-mah-chee-ah
delicatessen	**la salumeria**	lah sah-loo-meh-ree-ah
department store	**il grande magazzino**	eel gran-deh mag-gad-zee-noh
grocery	**alimentari**	ah-lee-men-tah-ree
hairdresser	**il parrucchiere**	eel par-oo-kee-air-eh
ice cream parlour	**la gelateria**	lah jel-lah-tair-ree-ah
market	**il mercato**	eel mair-kah-toh
newsstand	**l'edicola**	leh-dee-koh-lah
post office	**l'ufficio postale**	loo-fee-choh pos-tah-leh
supermarket	**il supermercato**	eel su-pair-mair-kah-toh
tobacconist	**il tabaccaio**	eel tah-bak-eye-oh
travel agency	**l'agenzia di viaggi**	lah-jen-tsee-ah dee vee-ad-jee

Sightseeing

art gallery	**la pinacoteca**	lah peena-koh-teh-kah
bus stop	**la fermata dell'autobus**	lah fair-mah-tah dell ow-toh-booss
church	**la chiesa**	lah kee-eh-zah
	la basilica	lah bah-seel-i-kah
closed for holidays	**chiuso per le ferie**	kee-oo-zoh pair leh fair-ee-eh
garden	**il giardino**	eel jar-dee-no
museum	**il museo**	eel moo-zeh-oh
railway station	**la stazione**	lah stah-tsee-oh-neh
tourist information	**l'ufficio di turismo**	loo-fee-choh dee too-ree-smoh

Staying in a Hotel

Do you have any vacant rooms?	**Avete camere libere?**	ah-veh-teh kah-mair-eh lee bair-eh?
double room	**una camera doppia**	oona kah-mair-ah doh-pee-ah
with double bed	**con letto matrimoniale**	kon let-toh mah-tree-moh-nee-ah-leh
twin room	**una camera con due letti**	oona kah-mair-ah kon doo-eh let-tee
single room	**una camera singola**	oona kah-mair-ah sing-goh-lah
room with a bath, shower	**una camera con bagno, con doccia**	oona kah-mair-ah kon ban-yoh, kon dot-chah
I have a reservation.	**Ho fatto una prenotazione.**	oh fat-toh oona preh-noh-tah-tsee-oh-neh

Eating Out

Have you got a table for ...?	**Avete una tavola per ... ?**	ah-veh-teh oona tah-voh-lah pair ...?
I'd like to reserve a table.	**Vorrei riservare una tavola.**	vor-ray ree-sair-vah-reh oona tah-voh-lah
breakfast	**colazione**	koh-lah-tsee-oh-neh
lunch	**pranzo**	pran-tsoh
dinner	**cena**	cheh-nah
The bill	**Il conto**	eel kon-toh
waitress	**cameriera**	kah-mair-ee-air-ah
waiter	**cameriere**	kah-mair-ee-air-eh
fixed price menu	**il menù a prezzo fisso**	eel meh-noo ah pret-soh fee-soh
dish of the day	**piatto del giorno**	pee-ah-toh dell jor-no
starter	**antipasto**	an-tee-pass-toh
first course	**il primo**	eel pree-moh
main course	**il secondo**	eel seh-kon-doh
vegetables	**contorni**	eel kon-tor-noh
dessert	**il dolce**	eel doll-cheh
cover charge	**il coperto**	eel koh-pair-toh
wine list	**la lista dei vini**	lah lee-stah day vee-nee
glass	**il bicchiere**	eel bee-kee-air-eh
bottle	**la bottiglia**	lah bot-teel-yah
knife	**il coltello**	eel kol-tell-oh
fork	**la forchetta**	lah for-ket-tah
spoon	**il cucchiaio**	eel koo-kee-eye-oh

Menu Decoder

l'acqua minerale gassata/ naturale	lah-kwah mee-nair-ah-leh gah-zah-tah/ nah-too-rah-leh	mineral water fizzy/still
agnello	ah-niell-oh	lamb
aglio	al-ee-oh	garlic
al forno	al for-noh	baked
alla griglia	ah-lah greel-yah	grilled
la birra	lah beer-rah	beer
la bistecca	lah bee-stek-kah	steak
il burro	eel boor-oh	butter
il caffè	eel kah-feh	coffee
la carne	la kar-neh	meat
carne di maiale	kar-neh dee mah-yah-leh	pork
la cipolla	la chip-oh-lah	onion
i fagioli	ee fah-joh-lee	beans
il formaggio	eel for-mad-joh	cheese
le fragole	lch frah goh lch	strawberries
il fritto misto	eel free-toh mees-toh	mixed fried dish
la frutta	la froot-tah	fruit
frutti di mare	froo-tee dee mah-reh	seafood
i funghi	ee foon-ghee	mushrooms
i gamberi	ee gam-bair-ee	prawns
il gelato	eel jel-lah-toh	ice cream
l'insalata	leen-sah-lah-tah	salad
il latte	eel laht-teh	milk
il manzo	eel man-tsoh	beef
l'olio	loh-lee-oh	oil
il pane	eel pah-neh	bread
le patate	leh pah-tah-teh	potatoes
le patatine	leh pah-tah-teen-eh	

fritte	free-teh	chips
il pepe	eel peh-peh	pepper
il pesce	eel pesh-eh	fish
il pollo	eel poll-oh	chicken
il pomodoro	eel poh-moh-dor-oh	tomato
il prosciutto cotto/crudo	eel pro-shoo-toh kot-toh/kroo-doh	ham cooked/cured
il riso	eel ree-zoh	rice
il sale	eel sah-leh	salt
la salsiccia	lah sal-see-chah	sausage
succo d'arancia/ di limone	soo-koh dah-ran-chah/ dee lee-moh-neh	orange/lemon juice
il tè	eel teh	tea
la torta	lah tor-tah	cake/tart
l'uovo	loo-oh-voh	egg
vino bianco	vee-noh bee-ang-koh	white wine
vino rosso	vee-noh ross-oh	red wine
le vongole	eel von-goh-leh	clams
lo zucchero	loh zoo-kair-oh	sugar
la zuppa	lah tsoo-pah	soup

Numbers

1	**uno**	oo-noh
2	**due**	doo-eh
3	**tre**	treh
4	**quattro**	kwat-roh
5	**cinque**	ching-kweh
6	**sei**	say-ee
7	**sette**	set-teh
8	**otto**	ot-toh
9	**nove**	noh-veh
10	**dieci**	dee-eh-chee
11	**undici**	oon-dee-chee
12	**dodici**	doh-dee-chee
13	**tredici**	tray-dee-chee
14	**quattordici**	kwat-tor-dee-chee
15	**quindici**	kwin-dee-chee
16	**sedici**	say-dee-chee
17	**diciassette**	dee-chah-set-teh
18	**diciotto**	dee-chot-toh
19	**diciannove**	dee-chah-noh-veh
20	**venti**	ven-tee
30	**trenta**	tren-tah
40	**quaranta**	kwah-ran-tah
50	**cinquanta**	ching-kwan-tah
60	**sessanta**	sess-an-tah
70	**settanta**	set-tan-tah
80	**ottanta**	ot-tan-tah
90	**novanta**	noh-van-tah
100	**cento**	chen-toh
1,000	**mille**	mee-leh
2,000	**duemila**	doo-eh-mee-lah
1,000,000	**un milione**	oon meel-yoh-neh

Time

one minute	**un minuto**	oon mee-noo-toh
one hour	**un'ora**	oon or-ah
a day	**un giorno**	oon jor-noh
Monday	**lunedì**	loo-neh-dee
Tuesday	**martedì**	mar-teh-dee
Wednesday	**mercoledì**	mair-koh-leh-dee
Thursday	**giovedì**	joh-veh-dee
Friday	**venerdì**	ven-air-dee
Saturday	**sabato**	sah-bah-toh
Sunday	**domenica**	doh-meh-nee-kah

Index to Main Streets